Great Grace *reflects sound teaching and wise counsel with scriptural grounding for each theme. The personal illustrations show that Merle has proven the insights that he shares. At the same time, the work is visionary as he progressively paints a picture of the Church being vibrant as each believer appropriates and acts with great faith. The chapters progressively build toward the fullness of this vision.*

—KEITH YODER
Ministry and Leadership Consultant

Read Great Grace *and discover how the Lord's abundant flow of grace will meet you right where you are, and then empower you beyond your own ability.*

—LARRY KREIDER
Author and DOVE International founder

Walking in the Power
of God's Abundant Supply

MERLE SHENK

House To House Publications
Lititz, Pennsylvania USA
www.h2hp.com

Great Grace
Walking in the Power of God's Abundant Supply
By Merle Shenk

Copyright © 2025 Merle Shenk

Published by
House to House Publications
11 Toll Gate Road, Lititz, PA 17543 USA
Telephone: 800.848.5892
www.h2hp.com

ISBN: 978-1-886973-79-4

Unless otherwise noted, all scripture is taken from the New King James Version®. (NKJV) Copyright © 1982 by Thomas Nelson. Used by permission. All rights reserved

All rights reserved. No portion of this book may be reproduced without the permission of the publisher.

DEDICATION

*To our DOVE International family
and the family of Christ around the world,
may you continue to thrive in God's Great Grace!*

ACKNOWLEDGMENTS

To my family and friends, thank you for your support!

I am especially grateful for my wife, Cheree. I could not have done this project without you.

To my editors, thank you for your dedication and input to help see this book to completion.

CONTENTS

Foreword 9

1. **Great Grace** 11
2. **God's Gift** 21
3. **The Kingdom Gospel** 31
4. **Empowering Grace** 49
5. **Accessing Grace** 61
6. **Faith and Grace** 69
7. **Growing in Grace** 87
8. **Specialized Grace** 109
9. **Trusting God's Grace** 123
10. **Remain in Grace** 137

Chapter Outlines 153

FOREWORD

Merle Shenk's book *Great Grace,* is a true gift to the body of Christ! This book is both distinctly biblical and profoundly practical. Merle draws from his own personal experiences of all he learned about God's limitless supply of grace as he ministered throughout the world. *Great Grace* contains truth and revelation that I have not read in other books.

For the past few years, I have had the personal experience of traveling with Merle as we have been together in ministry in many nations. Merle practices what he preaches. I have watched him live in the genuineness of the great grace that Jesus offers again and again.

Wherever you find yourself in this season of life, you will be blessed and encouraged by this book. Merle taps into a reality of grace that anyone can receive and experience in their lives. Read *Great Grace* and discover how the Lord's abundant flow of grace will meet you right where you are, and then empower you beyond your own ability. This book is life-changing!

Larry Kreider
Author and founder of DOVE International

CHAPTER ONE

Great Grace

Experiencing God's Grace

Experiencing powerful moments of divine encounters completely transforms the way we live. Even as a young man, I was aware that there was more in God than what I had already experienced. Since then I have had personal experiences that have shaped my own understanding of God's grace from a theological concept into a defining revelation that has changed how I live. This expression of grace is available to every believer! Time and again, I have encountered the Lord's limitless supply—His abundant flow of grace that meets me right where I am and empowers beyond my own ability. The good news is that this expression of grace is available to every believer!

One such moment came during a season of serving as a worship director in our church. This experience would become a foundational revelation of what is available through God's grace. It was an encounter that would forever shape my understanding of God's limitless supply available to all believers.

I was preparing for an upcoming time of ministry and had spent a significant amount of time in prayer and preparation.

Despite all of this, things were still not fully coming together. The weight of that uncertainty brought stress and I was experiencing an unusual amount of desperation. As I pressed into God in intercession and prayed in tongues, an unexpected shift occurred. A deep peace hit the core of my stomach. It was like receiving a substance in my spirit! This was the first of what would be many similar encounters. I have come to understand these encounters as moments when I would receive a supernatural portion of God's grace and empowerment by the Holy Spirit.

The experience was undeniable—tangible, almost physical. It was more than just peace; it was supply. In an instant, there was a deep knowing that everything I needed was already provided. Strangely, I did not have a clearer plan in mind, yet a fullness settled in my heart. It was a peace from God that confirmed something was imparted into my spirit. As the time of ministry unfolded, life from God's heart flowed in a profound and powerful way. Over time, these moments became recognizable as times of divine impartation—God downloading a portion of His grace, His supply, and His power.

Through repeated encounters, the ability to depend on and draw from God's grace grew. Powerful ministry times often followed, revealing that God was always faithful to provide exactly what was needed. I grew more and more confident in His provision. God's preparation always proved far greater than my human effort alone. It often met me when I felt poured out and like I had nothing left to give. I now prepare differently, posturing myself humbly as a ready vessel, prepared to receive and release what He has already supplied.

Over the years, my faith deepened in God's ability to deliver His empowering supply. The pursuit is to make room for His grace, power, and presence to move freely, both personally and through ministry to others. Without Him, nothing of true value can be accomplished; His leading is what sustains and directs every step.

Romans 13:14 says, "But put on the Lord Jesus Christ, and make no provision for the flesh, to fulfill its lusts." Paul instructs the church in Rome to put on Christ and not allow any space for the flesh to have its way. If provision can be made for the flesh, as Paul warns against, how much more can provision be made for the desires of the Holy Spirit to be fulfilled? The life flow of the Holy Spirit within a believer is sacred—more than just an anointing. It is an ever-present reality of His work available to every follower of Jesus.

It is important to be intentional about living in alignment with God's grace to avoid restricting the free flow of God's power in our lives. As followers of Christ, we have a responsibility to carry His life, love, and power to the world. The way we orient our lives, schedules and priorities—through surrender and dependence on Him—determines how freely His presence moves and ministers through us.

Reflection Questions

How does our understanding of God's grace impact our understanding of His provision and empowerment?

What practical steps can believers take to cultivate a lifestyle that aligns with and makes room for the flow of God's grace?

Great Grace was upon Them All

"And with great power the apostles gave witness to the resurrection of the Lord Jesus. And great grace was upon them all" (Acts 4:33).

In this verse, we see two key components at work. As the apostles preached, God's power bore witness to the resurrection of Jesus. But there was something else—great grace rested upon them all!

Was this a one-time encounter for the early church, or is it something we can experience today? The truth is, we can live in this reality—and many have. Throughout church history, countless moves of God have demonstrated that His great grace is still available!

It is possible to live out these realities in our own lives today! The testimony we read about from Acts 4, provides us with a glimpse into what a measure of heaven looks like when it touches earth.

Jesus taught us to pray in Matthew 6:10, "Let Your kingdom come, Let Your will be done, on earth as it is in heaven." He was not instructing believers to pray for something unattainable. He did not mean, "Pray this way, but in reality, you will never see it." Acts 4 provides a tangible manifestation, a scriptural picture of what happens when heaven invades earth.

The apostles leading the church at this time were the ones Jesus had personally taught to pray in this way. This is no coincidence. He not only instructed them in prayer but also modeled a life of unity with the Heavenly Father, that was empowered by the Holy Spirit.

In Acts 4, those who had walked with Jesus understood clearly what was available to the church. They had witnessed His ministry, experienced His mentorship, and seen His death, resurrection, and ascension. In obedience, they had waited in Jerusalem for the promise of the Father, which was the empowering baptism of the Holy Spirit.

These same disciples faced the chilling effects of persecution following the arrest of Peter and John. Yet, instead of retreating in fear, they gathered in prayer, acknowledging their struggles while standing firmly on the Word of God. As a result, they were filled again with the Holy Spirit and emboldened to continue their mission.

Acts 4:33-37 says, "And with great power the apostles gave witness to the resurrection of the Lord Jesus. And great grace was upon them all. Nor was there anyone among them who lacked; for all who were possessors of lands or houses sold them, and brought the proceeds of the things that were sold, and laid them at the apostles' feet; and they distributed to each as anyone had need. And Joseph, who was also named Barnabas by the apostles (which is translated Son of Encouragement), a Levite of the country of Cyprus, having land, sold it, and brought the money and laid it at the apostles' feet."

The results we see in verses 33-37 is a dynamic picture of God's power and grace moving among His people. Everyone was experiencing an amazing unity of heart and mind. They even saw resources being shared in such a way that would make a modern communist jealous. I am not suggesting that the church should sell everything and create communes. There have been enough experiments with that model to know it often leads to some strange places.

However, what stands out in this church community is the unprecedented abundance they experienced! What was noticeably absent was selfishness, self-preservation, and personal ambition. (Though these attitudes later surfaced with Ananias and Sapphira.) Instead, the church body experienced an overflow of blessing poured out in an atmosphere where brothers and sisters were united. They were of one heart and one mind in the Lord.

In this environment of unity, the apostles ministered the gospel with great power. Jaw-dropping miracles took place. People were hearing the gospel with signs and wonders following. We can see the results of great grace being upon everyone!

Every person living together under God's great grace caused abundance to flow so that there was more than enough to fill every need.

Reflection Questions

How does the unity of believers contribute to the manifestation of God's great grace and power in the church today?

What lessons can modern believers learn from the early church's experience in Acts 4 regarding generosity, unity, and the supernatural work of the Holy Spirit?

The Power of Grace Synergy

In this, I see the practical outworking of what Paul describes in 2 Corinthians 9:8 "And God is able to make all grace abound toward you, that you, always having all sufficiency in all things, may have an abundance for every good work."

The result of all grace abounding to us (and this sounds strikingly similar to "great grace was upon them all" as mentioned in Acts 4) is that we have all sufficiency in all things and have abundance so that every good work that God wants us to do can be accomplished! This scripture was written in the context of being a joyful giver. I don't think Paul was writing an empty promise or simply a hopeful encouragement. I believe that this was his lived experience.

In Philippians 4:12, Paul says that he knows how to be

abased and that he knows how to abound. Why is it so easy to focus on the abased part of this scripture and miss the fact that Paul says, "I know how to abound"?

To abound is more than just supernatural financial provision. It is a declaration that God's grace supplies whatever is needed to fulfill His purpose. Whether it is time, wisdom, strength, or resources, grace ensures that every good work can be accomplished. Everyone functioning in full grace releases such blessing through the body of Christ that there are simply no needs! There was plenty to go around.

In Acts 4, it does not appear that the land being sold was the only property these believers owned, leaving them in need themselves. Instead, the impression is that there was such a level of abundance that selling a portion of their property and giving the proceeds to the apostles was not a burden—it was simply a natural response. And this was not a one-time event; it happened multiple times, demonstrating a continual flow of generosity in the early church.

What strikes me about this passage is the synergy that grace created. It wasn't just a few wealthy individuals giving while others looked on. Everyone played a role.

The apostles led with boldness and power. Believers prayed and shared. The entire community functioned like a well-connected body. This is the beauty of grace at work—it activates every person. The stay-at-home parent, the entrepreneur, the student, the teacher, the CEO, the person who feels like they live in the background—all engaged, all having a part to play.

I am standing in faith for the body of Christ to experience this level of grace upon each person. When each person experiences God's empowering supply of abundance, grace begins to flow through a community. Every person starts to get caught up in it. Every person finds his or her place and starts to flourish. The body of Christ begins to function as it was designed—each part working together, creating momentum that cannot be manufactured by human effort. Each one is knit together by what every joint supplies. The environment of such a church community becomes dynamically alive with the power of the Holy Spirit. When the grace of the Lord in people's lives comes together, a divine synergy is created.

Imagine a movement where this kind of grace synergy touches every individual. Where competition fades, and collaboration rises. Where each believer's gifts are celebrated and honored. Where the gospel is proclaimed with power and lives are transformed as a result. This is the environment shaped by God's grace—where the Holy Spirit moves powerfully through a unified people. In this space, humble preparation blends with supernatural power, sparking exponential impact. When this happens, overflow is inevitable. Revival is in the air.

This lifestyle isn't reserved for a select few who have learned to live by faith and partner with God—it is available to every believer! When each person's gifts and strengths function together under the great grace of God, they form a powerful unity that reflects heaven on earth and advances God's kingdom across the nations.

I pray your faith is stirred for what God can do in our generation through the example shown to us in Acts 4:33. Dive in to explore the fullness of God's grace for your own life!

Reflection Questions

How does the concept of "grace synergy" in the early church apply to modern Christian communities, and what practical steps can believers take to cultivate it?

In what ways does living in God's abundant grace transform individual purpose and collective impact within the body of Christ?

CHAPTER TWO

God's Gift

Receiving the Gift of Grace

At first, because of how I encountered God's supernatural grace at work in my life, it seemed as though His grace came as a package. This was largely based on how I initially received it. While driving to share my faith, I would pray in tongues, surrendering in faith to what God wanted to do. "Praying through" until I received a tangible deposit in my spirit. It often felt as though something was placed deep within me. Where insecurity, fear, or the weight of responsibility once lingered, they were replaced with peace, a deep assurance, and an awareness of God's presence. Hebrews 12:1 came alive in those moments, affirming that faith is indeed the substance of things hoped for.

In Bible college, we were trained to be ready to minister at a moment's notice. We were taught to come prepared for every meeting, always ready to give an answer for the hope we have, as Peter instructs in 1 Peter 3:15. This is good practice for all believers!

"But in your hearts revere Christ as Lord. Always be prepared to give an answer to everyone who asks you to give the reason for the hope that you have. But do this with gentleness and respect" (I Peter 3:15 NIV).

This practice of preparedness instilled in us the habit of living a prepared life, one where we always had something to give spiritually. Whether or not we were scheduled to preach, lead, or minister, we came to the Lord's table with something to share. That foundation of preparation, study, and love for God's Word and presence shaped me for ministry and has served me well over the years.

Years ago, while in an African country, I was being driven from one church meeting to another. After a full day of ministry, including preaching at two services and visiting homes to pray for the sick, we were now on our way to an evening church service. I apologized to my friends in the car, explaining that I wouldn't be very talkative. Exhausted and uncertain about what I was going to preach, I closed my eyes, leaned against the side of the car, and silently poured out my heart to the Lord in prayer. After several minutes, I experienced a strengthening from Him. With that strengthening came clear direction. Several scriptures were highlighted in my heart, and I quickly wrote them down and looked them up. That night, we experienced a powerful move of God's presence.

As we continue, I will unpack how my understanding of God's grace developed beyond a "package" mentality. But first, we need to look at some powerful foundational truths!

Christianity 101

When you hear the word grace, what comes to mind? For many, it is salvation. And that is absolutely right. Salvation is the entry point, the beginning of our encounter with grace. But salvation is far from the whole picture. Grace is not a one-time experience in which we surrender our lives to Jesus. It unfolds, saturating, transforming, and empowering every part of life.

To grasp this fully, we must first understand how grace operates at the moment of salvation. From there, we can explore how it carries us beyond that initial encounter at salvation.

"For by grace you have been saved through faith, and that not of yourselves; it is the gift of God, not of works, lest anyone should boast" (Ephesians 2:8-9).

Grace can be simply defined as God's work: what He does and what He supplies. Salvation is received by His grace through faith. This free gift is not earned but given in response to simple trust in Him.

A helpful comparison is often made between God's grace and His mercy. Mercy is not getting what we deserve, while grace goes even further by giving us what we do not deserve.

Imagine standing in traffic court with no money after being caught speeding, perhaps while rushing to an important appointment. The judge declares, "Guilty." But then he extends mercy: "Your fine is far beyond what you can pay, but my son has offered to cover the cost, so I will let you go." That is mercy. Then the judge continues, "Not only that, but I will also provide you with a personal rideshare service and driver for the rest of your life, free of charge. And here is a brand-new watch so you will never be late again." That is grace!

How crazy would that be? Mercy meant not getting what was deserved—the fine should have been paid. But grace went even further, providing free transportation for life and a new watch. You had done nothing to earn that gift from the judge.

This is a picture of the free gift of salvation received by God's grace. A powerful example of this is seen during Jesus' crucifixion. One of the thieves beside Him recognized that Jesus had done nothing wrong and asked to be remembered when He came into His kingdom. Jesus' response was stunning: "Today you will be with me in paradise" (Luke 23:41-43).

That thief had no opportunity to do anything good for God. Yet, because of simple faith in Jesus, he encountered God's grace.

This is amazing. This is scandalous. The thief on the cross had no chance to live a righteous life or accomplish anything significant for God. His story reveals the extravagant nature of grace and the goodness of God toward us—not because of anything we can do for Him, but because of His love for us.

One of the members of our church shared a testimony about when he first came to the Lord. He was in prison awaiting trial for a serious crime. While in prison he gave his life to Jesus. One night he had a dream in which Jesus came to him and said, "I am going to set you free, but I want you to serve me." Within the week his case was unexpectedly dismissed and he was set free from prison. The last time I heard from him, he was serving as a pastor in another church. He experienced the amazing grace of Jesus that was far better than he could have imagined.

This example of grace is confrontational to the religious mind-set. A religious mind-set seeks to earn righteousness through works, but God's grace operates differently. This kind of grace can make those who trust in their own good deeds, as if they can earn approval from God, feel uncomfortable. Some struggle to accept that a person could be saved in his or her dying moments simply by turning to Jesus–yet this is the radical, unearned nature of salvation.

"That's not fair!," they argue.

Grace isn't fair—it's good. It is the goodness of God on display for every person who responds to Him.

Right standing with God comes through His grace. Jesus took our punishment upon Himself on the cross, making a way for us to be restored to relationship with Him. Paul expresses this in Philippians 3:9, saying he does not rely on his own righteousness but receives the righteousness of Christ.

You are loved and chosen by God because of what He has done. Our righteousness is not earned. It is a gift by His grace. Now we have the opportunity to live out the righteousness that we are given.

Reflection Questions

How can the example of the thief on the cross help you understand and share the radical nature of God's grace with others?

How does the distinction between mercy and grace change your understanding of salvation?

Why do you think grace is often challenging for those with a religious mind-set to accept?

God's Grace Is Not Based Upon Feelings

This gift almost seems too good to be true! At times, in our journey of faith we encounter discouragement. Perhaps some may even feel discouraged right now. Doubts can creep in, making it hard to believe in God's love. Feelings of unworthiness, of not measuring up, not being good enough, righteous enough, or spiritual enough, can weigh heavily on the heart.

John Newton, the slave trader turned hymn writer, struggled with self-doubt and shame over his past life. He wrestled with the question of whether someone as sinful as him could be redeemed by God. He says: "I thought that surely the Scripture proved that there never was, nor could be, such a sinner as myself." [1]

Yet after encountering God's grace one stormy night, he penned one of the most famous hymns known in Christendom, "Amazing Grace, how sweet the sound that saved a wretch like me…" Though it took a while, he would eventually go on to fight against the very slave trade that he had been a part of in his previous years.

God's Gift

The Apostle John addresses this struggle of the heart in Scripture. In 1 John 3:20, he writes, "For if our heart condemns us, God is greater than our heart, and knows all things."

The Passion Translation puts it this way:

"Whenever our hearts make us feel guilty and remind us of our failures, we know that God is much greater and more merciful than our conscience, and he knows everything there is to know about us" {1 John 3:20 TPT}.

This is a powerful truth. The God who knows everything, past, present, and future, extends salvation by grace. His love is not based on human effort but on His own goodness. No condemnation from others, the devil, or even personal insecurities can outweigh the grace of God. That is His nature. That is His goodness.

The enemy works tirelessly to convince believers that this grace is too good to be true. He uses condemnation, guilt, shame, and fear to plant doubt. When these lies take root, the thought arises: "I'm not good enough for God." Striving to earn righteousness in human strength becomes the focus, yet Scripture declares that righteousness is a gift given at the very moment of faith in Jesus as Lord.

One preacher put it well: "Believers need to stop trying to get something that they already have!" The reality is that in Christ, righteousness is already secured.

Too often, feelings are given more weight than God's Word. Steve, a friend of mine, wisely notes, "Our feelings do not tell us what is true. They only tell us what we believe to be true."

When the church fails to stand on the truth of God's Word, insecurity, condemnation, and oppression take hold. That is not the life believers are called to live. The church is not called to be insecure or weighed down by guilt and shame. Through God's grace, complete freedom is available. Believers are empowered to fulfill His purpose, walking in the fullness of His grace, never bound by sin again.

Reflection Questions

In what areas of your life have you struggled to fully embrace the concept of grace; thinking instead that you must earn God's approval?

How can you shift your perspective from striving in your own strength to resting in the truth of God's grace and righteousness?

New Identity in Christ

The reality of God's grace is that we do not remain sinners. When we surrender to the lordship of Jesus Christ, the old man of sin is dead, buried with Christ, and we are made new in Him. We come alive spiritually. It is our new rebirth date. We are new creations in Him. As a new creation, we begin learning to live out the righteousness that was given to us. We are no longer sinners; we are sons and daughters of God.

Being a child of God, saved by His grace, is our new automatic default starting position. This means that on my best day, I am a child of God. On my worst day, I am still a child of God. When facing the hardest challenges, the biggest frustrations, or even great failures, we remain His children. There is always something to celebrate because God's gift is not dependent on us; it is dependent on Him. Salvation, by God's grace, is the foundation of the believer's life. It is secure.

Sometimes, it may feel like going back to the beginning, as if returning to the starting point in a board game. Even after a rough day, salvation remains intact. Praise Jesus, we are saved by His grace! We are no longer sinners.

We can still remember the old man. There is an awareness of once being spiritually dead and alienated from God. Paul speaks of this in Ephesians 2: "You who were dead in trespasses and sins…" The reality is that we used to be sinners, but the blood of Jesus has set us free. The grace of God has made us alive.

But for what purpose?

To live in relationship with God and demonstrate His kingdom to the world. Our lives are meant to be a testimony of His goodness and His intent for humanity. As Ephesians 2:10 declares: "For we are His workmanship, created in Christ Jesus for good works, which God prepared beforehand that we should walk in them."

The gospel is not just salvation from sin. While that is crucial, it is only the beginning. The gospel is the full revelation of God's will for mankind.

When many Christians speak of the gospel and salvation, they often focus on the forgiveness of sins. While that is true, it is not the whole picture. The gospel starts with salvation, but it encompasses so much more than that.

Reflection Questions

How does understanding your identity as a new creation in Christ influence the way you live?

What does it mean to walk in the "good works" that God has prepared for us, as mentioned in Ephesians 2:10?

ENDNOTES

1. https://www.museumofthebible.org/a-wretch-like-me

CHAPTER THREE

The Kingdom Gospel

The Gospel of the Kingdom

"Go therefore and make disciples of all the nations, baptizing them in the name of the Father and of the Son and of the Holy Spirit" (Matthew 28:19).

The Bible uses several Greek words for the word baptism. One of the words means "to dip in water, as if to wash something." But the word used for baptism in Matthew 28:19 and Mark 16:16, is the Greek word *baptizo*; it means more than just washing. It implies a full and constant submersion into the Father, Son and Holy Spirit.

"He who believes and is baptized will be saved; but he who does not believe will be condemned" (Mark 16:16).

I like to use the following illustration to describe this definition of baptism. A cucumber is placed into a vinegar solution until it is fully changed into a pickle. The cucumber sits in that solution, fully submerged, and in this process the whole cucumber becomes dramatically altered. The way it looks has changed, the way it smells has changed and the way it tastes has changed. It is still a cucumber, but it has been completely transformed.

This gives us a picture of the concept of baptism. We are to be fully submerged in God until we are changed completely. When people interact with us, the experience that they have with us is totally different than they would have had before we surrendered to Christ. When we become followers of Jesus, we can stop short of full transformation and settle for just agreeing intellectually to the knowledge of Christ. But that is not the goal! There must be a union with God, a real change, much like the change that takes place when a cucumber turns into a pickle! [1]

This is an example of what it will look like as our lives are fully surrendered under the King's domain or His kingdom. Every aspect of our life will be touched and fully affected by God's reign in our life.

Jesus preached the gospel of the kingdom before He ever went to the cross. Consider this passage:

"Now after John was put in prison, Jesus came to Galilee, preaching the gospel of the kingdom of God, and saying, 'The time is fulfilled, and the kingdom of God is at hand. Repent and believe in the gospel'" (Mark 1:14-15).

What gospel did Jesus preach? Today, much of the preaching of the gospel sounds something like this: God is your heavenly Father who loves you and has a plan for your life. He has a way for you to live. Turn away from your self-willed way of life, surrender to Him, and commit to following His ways.

Is this what Jesus preached?

Yes, that is part of what He preached. But His message went even deeper. His preaching was not limited to personal spirituality; it touched every area of life with practical examples of walking in God's ways.

A parallel verse in Matthew 4 further illustrates this: "And Jesus went about all Galilee, teaching in their synagogues, preaching the gospel of the kingdom, and healing all kinds of sickness and all kinds of disease among the people" (Matthew 4:23).

Before Jesus went to the cross, He was already preaching the gospel. But He didn't just preach it, He modeled it. In addition to preaching He healed the sick, restored the broken, and demonstrated what life could be like in relationship with the Father, fully submitted to His reign and kingdom.

In the Garden of Eden, mankind rejected God's rule by choosing their own way. The only restriction given to Adam and Eve was not to eat from the tree of the knowledge of good and evil. Yet Satan, appearing as a serpent, deceived them by suggesting that God had ulterior, evil motives. He convinced them that God was, somehow, holding out on them. He implied that God's ways were restrictive and that true enlightenment could only come by taking control of their own knowledge of good and evil.

He implied that God was suppressing them, keeping them from becoming something much better than they were, keeping them from becoming like God Himself. This deception led them to believe that God was not good, that He was withholding something from them, and that His instructions on how to live could not be trusted.

These same lies persist today. Modern philosophies claim that God's ways are outdated and restrictive, preventing humanity from somehow reaching their full potential. Some go so far as to suggest that mankind must free itself from God's influence to attain a higher level of understanding. Some of the most extreme ideologies argue that truth is relative and that humanity is evolving beyond God's design for male and female, redefining fundamental aspects of identity. These thoughts represent some of the most extreme deviations from the way God has designed the human experience in our world today. However, in reality, these false ideas, that God is not good, that His rulership is corrupt, that His ways are restrictive and cannot be trusted, are simply repackaged versions of the same deception Satan used in Eden.

Interestingly, Satan did not try to persuade Adam and Eve to follow him as their god. He merely had to convince them to reject God's truth and rely on their own understanding. Under his influence, they rejected God's reign and determined that they should try to become their own master by knowing good and evil themselves. The result was the entrance of sin and death into the world. Humanity experienced separation from God and His kingdom for the first time.

Yet God, in His mercy, did not want mankind to live in this fallen state forever. To prevent them from being eternally separated from Him, He removed them from Eden and blocked access to the tree of life (Genesis 3:22). Over time, He spoke to prophets and leaders, establishing the Old Covenant to prepare the way for humanity's return to Him. He chose a people for Himself and gave them His law, knowing that many would still reject His reign. Despite mankind's unfaithfulness, God continued reaching out through the ages.

As history unfolded, humanity's fallen nature led to the distortion of God's laws. The Old Covenant became entangled in man-made traditions, rules, and religious systems that centralized power in the hands of religious leaders in the name of God. Jesus confronted this corruption, as seen in Matthew 23:13:

"But woe to you, scribes and Pharisees, hypocrites! For you shut up the kingdom of heaven against men; for you neither go in yourselves, nor do you allow those who are entering to go in."

This was the state of the world when Jesus came preaching the gospel of the kingdom. The term gospel means "good news." His message called people to turn away from self-rule and return to God's reign, undoing the very choice Adam and Eve made in the garden. Because of His sacrifice on the cross, the consequences of that original rebellion could be reversed.

Today, many still reject God as their ruler. They dismiss His ways and, as a result, experience brokenness in the world caused by mankind trying to rule themselves without God. The call to preach the gospel remains the same: to turn people back to the lordship of Jesus. Like Jesus, we are called not only to preach but to demonstrate the gospel, showing an alternative way of life, not one of religious rules, but a life empowered by God's grace.

Reflection Questions

How does understanding Jesus' preaching of the kingdom, which he did before he died on the cross, challenge or expand your view of the gospel and its impact on everyday life?

What are some practical ways to live under God's reign in daily life?

Living the Full Gospel of the Kingdom

Jesus was demonstrating the gospel of the kingdom. He was modeling what a life surrendered to the will of God looked like. He was showing what it meant to live from a place of relationship with God the Father. His life was the visible example of the gospel of God for mankind, making it clear for all to see. Everything He preached and demonstrated shows us the fullness of the gospel.

Everything Jesus taught about God and His kingdom is the Good News, the gospel of the kingdom of God! He revealed an accurate picture of God's heart for mankind so people could see and know that God is good and trustworthy. His message countered the lies of the enemy, rejecting the false narrative that God could not be trusted or that He had ulterior motives. Jesus' example makes it desirable for people to trust their lives to God and make Him their King.

This revelation of God's love, His goodness, and His will for mankind directly contradicted the deception of Satan. It also challenged the rigid, distorted image of God presented by the religious systems of the time. As one preacher put it, "Jesus is everything that God has to say about Himself." Through Jesus, it became clear that God's intention for mankind was good, His Word was true, and He was able to fulfill His promises.

What if we had a record of Jesus' actual words while He was preaching these things? We do! When we understand that everything Jesus said in Matthew, Mark, Luke, and John is the gospel of how God created mankind to live under His rule, it adds a new dimension to what we read. All of it is the gospel. Take, for example, the Sermon on the Mount in Matthew chapters 5, 6, and 7. Everything Jesus taught in those chapters is a revelation of God's will for what it looks like to live in His kingdom with Him as our King.

Below is a summary of Matthew chapters 5, 6, and 7 in my own words. This is not meant to replace the Scriptures in any way, but rather to highlight the themes in the order Jesus preached them. Each of these themes paints a practical picture of what it looks like to live under God's reign.

Matthew 5-7 in my own words

Those who live this way will experience tremendous blessing. When you recognize your need for God's rulership and leadership in your life, you will experience the blessing of having it. You will experience the blessing of comfort when you mourn, and be blessed with inheriting the earth when you live meekly. There is the blessing of more than enough righteousness for those who really desire it. When you give mercy you will be blessed in getting it in return. Keeping your heart pure and undefiled will bring the blessing of seeing God. When you work to make peace, you will be blessed by being known by His name. When you are persecuted for doing what is right, you will be blessed to experience the resources of heaven at your disposal.

There are heavenly rewards heaped up for those who are wrongly treated for Jesus' sake. This is actually a reason to celebrate. Your presence in the world will give it flavor and help preserve it. You will cause others to be able to see and your good works will cause them to direct glory to God.

Jesus came to fulfill every single detail of the law. Each detail is important and valuable to be taught. All God's commands are important and you will be known in heaven by how you keep them. You will have to receive your righteousness in a better way than the scribes and Pharisees to get into heaven's kingdom.

Keep your heart pure; you will be judged if you foster anger in your heart. Making right with the brother you offended is higher priority than your generosity towards God. Make it right first then come back and give to God. Be diligent to settle with your adversary without delay. Ignoring them will be painful and costly.

Keep your life clean and holy. Keep your heart pure from adulterous thoughts. Sins of the heart are costly; remove from your life that which causes sin. Don't break your marriage covenant. Let your yes be yes and no be no; be a person of your word.

Don't live the way the world does. Don't retaliate when someone wrongs you, even if they do it again. When someone wants to take something from you, give them more. When you are forced to do something, do more than what is required. Be readily available to people. Generously give, when people ask and loan, when people need to borrow. Love, bless, do good, and pray for your enemies. Be perfect like God, in that you treat others based on who you are, not based on how they act.

God rewards those who secretly give to those in need. Your secret life of prayer and fasting will be blessed in an obvious way. Forgive people, and when you wrong someone, make it right as quickly as you can.

Use finances to build wealth in heaven, where it lasts eternally. Money can direct the passion of your heart, so serve God with it.

Keep your perspective on life clear and healthy, rooted in God's viewpoint. It will affect every other area of your life.

You can only serve one master. It will either be God or riches. You choose which one you are going to love.

You will either use riches to serve God or you will try to use God to serve riches.

Don't live a life of worry and anxiety. Know your value to God and learn how He takes care of His creation. Allow this to give you faith for how He will provide for you. Put His kingdom and righteousness first and all the things others strive for will be added to you. He gives you everything that you need to deal with the challenges of today. Don't let the uncertainty of the future cloud your focus for today.

Don't set yourself up as a judge. Don't be hypocritically blind to your own shortcomings, but work on your life first then help others. Honor what is holy by using it wisely and keep your best for those who will appreciate it.

Know your value as a child of God. Keep asking, keep seeking, keep knocking, God will give you what you need. Consider how you treat your own children and remember that God is an even better parent than you are. Treat others the way you would like to be treated.

Enter through the narrow gate and remain on the narrow way, no matter how hard it is.

Beware of people who use prophecy to serve themselves and gain advantage over others. The fruit of their life is obvious. Know the fruit of those who prophesy and speak into your life.

Reject lawlessness, follow God's will and pursue truly knowing Him. Simply doing good works and miracles in God's name is not enough to enter the kingdom of heaven.

Everyone who hears these authoritative teachings of Jesus, and responds by orienting their life around them, is wise and will have a solid foundation. No matter what comes against them, they will still be standing. Whoever hears these authoritative teachings and does not orient their life around them, no matter how grand their life looks, will not withstand the storms of life.

Wow, what an all-encompassing message of Jesus! This is just a brief attempt at summarizing these chapters; entire books have been written on just these three chapters. And there is so much more that we have a record of Jesus saying and doing. What a complete picture of what living the gospel in the kingdom of God truly looks like. This is a glimpse of the full gospel of the kingdom that Jesus was preaching.

Reflection Questions

How does understanding the Sermon on the Mount, as part of the full gospel of the kingdom Jesus preached, challenge the way you live?

What practical steps can you take to align your daily life with the teachings of the Sermon on the Mount?

The Full Picture of Biblical Salvation

Biblically, salvation is experienced as we respond to the full message of the gospel of God's kingdom. It encompasses more than just the cross and the removal of sin. Before you react to that statement, allow me to explain. While countless books have been written on this topic, understanding a brief overview is key to grasping God's saving grace and how it actively works in our lives.

When we study the doctrine of salvation in Scripture, we clearly see three parts to it:

JUSTIFICATION happens instantly at the very moment we turn our lives over to Jesus as our Lord and Savior. We are made just and righteous before God. The Holy Spirit breathes life into our spirit, and we become spiritually alive. This is what most people think of when they talk about salvation. We are delivered from eternal death and separation from God. As discussed earlier, we are not justified by our own works but by His grace alone.

SANCTIFICATION is not instant, but it is part of what the Bible describes as salvation. It is a lifelong process of being a disciple of Jesus and following Him. It is living our lives in obedience and alignment with His kingdom. This is the part of salvation that we actively work out on a daily basis, sometimes wrestling with it through challenges and struggles.

The Apostle Paul speaks of this in Philippians 2:12, "Therefore, my beloved, as you have always obeyed, not as in my presence only, but now much more in my absence, work out your own salvation with fear and trembling."

Sanctification is the process of transformation that we encounter as we walk in relationship with God. Romans 12:2 (NIV) reinforces this: "Do not conform to the pattern of this world, but be transformed by the renewing of your mind. Then you will be able to test and approve what God's will is—his good, pleasing and perfect will."

Sanctification is the salvation of our soul whereby our mind, will, and emotions are renewed by interaction with God's grace. As we continually engage with Jesus, we are changed by the power of the Holy Spirit and begin to reflect Him in our world.

2 Corinthians 3:18 describes this process: "But we all, with unveiled face, beholding as in a mirror the glory of the Lord, are being transformed into the same image from glory to glory, just as by the Spirit of the Lord."

This part of salvation is a journey in which we grow in wisdom and obedience to Jesus. As we align our lives with His will, we develop a deeper and more effective prayer life, learning to ask according to His heart. Because we live surrendered under His rulership, keeping His commandments and doing what pleases Him, we receive what we ask.

1 John 3:22 affirms this: "And whatever we ask we receive from Him, because we keep His commandments and do those things that are pleasing in His sight."

Jesus prayed for this process in John 17:17-19: "Sanctify them by Your truth. Your word is truth. As You sent Me into the world, I also have sent them into the world. And for their sakes I sanctify Myself, that they also may be sanctified by the truth."

Jesus lived a life of obedience to the Father's will not for His own sake but for our sake. This is what He means when He says, "for their sakes I sanctify Myself," not that He was not perfect already but He was demonstrating the process of sanctification to the disciples.

Paul also describes this journey in 1 Corinthians 3:10-17. He explains that the foundation of Christ has been laid in the lives of believers, but they must build upon it. The quality of what they build with (gold, silver, precious stones, or wood, straw, and stubble) will be tested by fire. This illustrates the process of sanctification. Justification ensures salvation into eternity because of turning to God, but sanctification is the growth journey we go on as we live out that salvation in obedience to Christ.

Sanctification is biblically part of salvation, and God's grace is what empowers us in this process. Grace is not a one-time event at justification; it is an ongoing flow of divine empowerment that helps us grow into Christlikeness.

1 John 4:17 highlights this transformation: "Love has been perfected among us in this: that we may have boldness in the day of judgment; because as He is, so are we in this world."

GLORIFICATION The third part of salvation is the glorification of our bodies, which will happen in the future at

Christ's return. On that day, we will receive glorified bodies, transformed by God's power.

Paul speaks of this in 1 Corinthians 15:42-43, "So also is the resurrection of the dead. The body is sown in corruption, it is raised in incorruption. It is sown in dishonor, it is raised in glory. It is sown in weakness, it is raised in power."

He continues in 1 Corinthians 15:51-53: "Behold, I tell you a mystery: We shall not all sleep, but we shall all be changed— in a moment, in the twinkling of an eye, at the last trumpet. For the trumpet will sound, and the dead will be raised incorruptible, and we shall be changed. For this corruptible must put on incorruption, and this mortal must put on immortality."

Philippians 3:21 also describes this future transformation: "Who will transform our lowly body that it may be conformed to His glorious body, according to the working by which He is able even to subdue all things to Himself."

For the purposes of this discussion, we will not go further into the theme of glorification, but it is an essential part of our ultimate salvation.

The Three Parts of Biblical Salvation

Biblically, salvation is a complete picture of God's goodness and His will brought into our lives by His reign. It is us living fully alive in His kingdom. These three parts—justification, sanctification, and glorification—together form the full picture of salvation for spirit, soul, and body. Justification is instant, sanctification is a continual process, and glorification is our eternal future.

John references all three parts of salvation in 1 John 3:2-3. Italicized words are my interjections: "Beloved, now we are children of God; *(justification)* and it has not yet been revealed what we shall be, but we know that when He is revealed, we shall be like Him *(glorification)*, for we shall see Him as He is. And everyone who has this hope in Him purifies himself *(sanctification)*, just as He is pure."

Paul also references these three aspects in 1 Thessalonians 5:23: "Now may the God of peace Himself sanctify you completely; and may your whole spirit *(justification)*, soul *(sanctification)*, and body *(glorification)* be preserved blameless at the coming of our Lord Jesus Christ."

Why is this important? Because grace does not only supply justification but the full picture of salvation. Grace is the constant flow of God's love, salvation, and power, shaping believers into the image of Christ, ensuring freedom, victory, and continual renewal. It is the unshakable foundation of the Christian life.

God's grace is the full supply of what we need to live, grow, and accomplish everything He has called us to do. It is not a one-time event but a constant flow of divine empowerment that starts the moment we surrender to Jesus and continues throughout eternity.

Reflection Questions

How does understanding the three parts of salvation—justification, sanctification, and glorification—impact your perspective of salvation?

In what ways do you see God's grace actively working in your daily process of sanctification?

ENDNOTE

1. James Montgomery Boice, *Bible Study Magazine*, May 1989. (Olive Tree Enhanced Strong's Dictionary)

Great Grace

CHAPTER FOUR

Empowering Grace

Grace in Every Season

I learned more and more about the power of God's grace while leading ministry through hardships and trials. God guided us through difficult seasons. He provided direction even when we were dealing with deep hurt and disappointment. There were times when we were tempted to give in and accept a victim mind-set because of the challenges we faced. Yet, God sent people into our lives to encourage us and help us walk through to the other side. Many times, we experienced God's empowering grace to minister to others, even when our own emotions were grieving or overwhelmed with frustration.

God's grace is present even in trials and pain. His grace does not depend on ideal circumstances; it remains available to strengthen, sustain, and guide us no matter what we face.

God's grace is not just for spiritual matters; it extends to practical, everyday challenges as well. I remember times when God provided solutions to problems that had nothing to do with ministry. One day, I was on the phone with someone on the other side of the world listening to the details of a maintenance issue they were facing. Suddenly, I knew in my spirit what the problem was as well as the solution. This was not a natural troubleshooting skill, it was a gut-level knowing from the Lord. It was a conviction coupled with the wisdom of God in my heart.

God had given me a word of knowledge about what was wrong and how to fix it. Later, the person I spoke with called to say, "I should have just listened to you immediately. I spent a lot of money replacing and checking other things, but in the end, the issue was exactly what you suggested." The problem turned out to be an obscure mechanical piece—a solution that was not obvious but was completely accurate.

This type of thing has happened to me multiple times, I recognize these moments as God's leading, not through my own wisdom or strength, but through the overflow of His grace.

We have the opportunity to experience God's grace in every area of our lives. The work and leading of the Holy Spirit are part of His grace. There is a throne of grace that we can approach with boldness and confidence in any time of need! As the writer of Hebrews tells us in Hebrews 4:16, this grace is not just for what we traditionally view as "ministry." When we live with our hearts aligned with God's, we have His help in every situation. His grace is truly the divine advantage!

Reflection Questions

How have you experienced God's grace in difficult or unexpected situations?

In what ways can recognizing God's grace in daily life strengthen your faith and trust in Him?

The Live Wire of God's Grace

Is grace like a gift box from heaven that needs to be unwrapped, opened up, and explored? That was once my perspective. It seemed that when a person gave their life to Jesus, God handed them a supernatural package, hovering over their life like a special "power-up" ability in a video game. This package, representing God's grace, contained not only salvation but also everything needed to accomplish His calling: power, authority, and supernatural gifting.

But over time, a better metaphor emerged. The grace of God truly does carry all of these things into the life of the believer, but it is not merely a package waiting to be unwrapped. Instead, grace is a constant, active force—a divine flow of power and life. The very first thing we experience from God's grace is our sins being washed away by the blood of Jesus.

A live electrical wire from heaven serves as a better illustration. Just as an electrical appliance remains lifeless until plugged into a power source, so too is a person spiritually dead until connected to Jesus. Through repentance and surrender, the life-giving flow of the Holy Spirit is encountered. From that moment, we have access to everything needed to accomplish God's will. Grace is not a one-time gift; it is an ongoing, ever-present flow.

Sanctification, the process of transformation into becoming more like Jesus, is also part of God's grace. Paul tells Titus that grace actually teaches believers how to live.

"For the grace of God that brings salvation has appeared to all men, teaching us that, denying ungodliness and worldly lusts, we should live soberly, righteously, and godly in the present age, looking for the blessed hope and glorious appearing of our great God and Savior Jesus Christ" (Titus 2:11-13).

Paul is saying that grace itself provides instruction for godly living. But how does grace teach? Isn't that the role of the Holy Spirit? Yes! The Holy Spirit is the One who teaches, leads, and empowers, and receiving the Holy Spirit is part of God's grace. In fact, the writer of Hebrews calls the Holy Spirit the "Spirit of grace" (Hebrews 10:29). The work of the Holy Spirit in the life of the believer cannot be separated from the grace of God.

Many today desire the morality and goodness that come from a Christian worldview, but attempt to live it out without submitting to God. Trying to follow Jesus' teachings in human strength, apart from His empowering grace, leads to discouraged striving or dead religion. When attempting to accomplish God's will through human effort alone, there is a risk of falling into the legalism of dead works. People may know what they ought to do, but be unable to live it out. This leads to shame or hypocrisy. Both attempts focus on external works while missing the supernatural transformation that only grace can bring. This happens when a relational connection with God is neglected.

Knowing what is right from Scripture and personal understanding is not enough. Without a life-giving relationship with the Holy Spirit self efforts can become a burden of striving and performance. If we are not careful, spiritual life becomes driven by duty rather than delight. Guilt, fear, and obligation start to creep in, and actions are motivated by pressure rather than joy. This is the birthplace of dead religious works: tedious actions that lack faith and life.

Another powerful metaphor for this can be found in the two trees in the Garden of Eden. Attempting to do God's will in human strength is like choosing to eat from the tree of the knowledge of good and evil rather than the tree of life. The tree of life represents a connected relationship with Jesus—living from a place of union with Him. The tree of knowledge of good and evil represents taking control, determining right and wrong independently from God, and striving through intellect and willpower. One aspect of this self-reliance is a sense of religious duty that is driven by shame, guilt, or fear rather than love and grace that comes from a life connected to Jesus.

There is a choice: to live from a place of relationship with God, strengthened by His grace, or to live from a place of striving and relying on personal strength. Humanity has excelled at creating elaborate systems to define good and avoid evil. Even as a believer, it is possible to fall into the trap of trying to please God through self-effort rather than through grace.

The grace of God flows from a personal connection and relationship with Him. It is not just an external power—it is God's divine life, empowering believers to accomplish His will, His way, in unity with Him.

Reflection Questions

Are you living from a place of duty or are you living from a place of delight?

Have you experienced the grace of the Holy Spirit teaching you how to follow God's will?

The River and the Trees

Another way to understand God's grace is to see it as a river. It constantly flows from Him as the Source. As it reaches our lives, we have the choice of how deep we want to go. We can stay in the shallows, splashing around, or we can dive in and be carried by its current.

Ezekiel describes a prophetic encounter with a river flowing from the throne of God in Ezekiel 47. Could he have been seeing a vision of God's provision of grace flowing out to the nations? Verse 9 tells us that "everything will live wherever the river flows." Ezekiel also speaks of the healing that is experienced wherever the river touches and describes trees that draw nourishment from it the river. These trees bear fruit continually, their leaves will not wither. Their fruit will be for food and their leaves will bring healing to the nations. This passage paints a powerful picture of the river as an abundant supply of grace that flows from God's throne providing vitality and resources to His kingdom.

What a unique and specific image! These trees, rooted by the river, are not just bearing fruit once a year in a short season, but are continually producing month by month. This principle of continual harvest reveals the supernatural work of God's grace. His river supplies unending life and provision, bringing healing and transformation wherever it flows. As believers, we are called to be like those trees—drawing from the river, thriving, producing fruit, and becoming a source of nourishment and healing for the nations.

The Holy Spirit is part of this abundant grace. No wonder Jesus proclaimed in John 7:37, "If anyone thirsts, let him come to Me and drink." He is the source of the river of God's grace.

Jesus then declares:

""He who believes in Me, as the Scripture has said, out of his heart will flow rivers of living water.' But this He spoke concerning the Spirit, whom those believing in Him would receive" (John 7:38-39a).

The work of the Holy Spirit, flowing through our hearts, is part of God's grace. He brings refreshing, life, joy, and strength—first to us, and then through us to others. Because we are connected to Jesus, the Holy Spirit flows through us to the world around us.

Psalm 46:4 beautifully describes this river: "There is a river whose streams shall make glad the city of God, The holy place of the tabernacle of the Most High."

One of my favorite passages reveals the result of rejecting worldly influence and delighting in the Lord. The one who does this is compared to a deeply rooted, fruit-bearing tree that prospers in everything he does:

"Blessed is the man who walks not in the counsel of the ungodly, nor stands in the path of sinners, nor sits in the seat of the scornful; but his delight is in the law of the LORD, and in His law he meditates day and night. He shall be like a tree planted by the rivers of water, that brings forth its fruit in its season, whose leaf also shall not wither; And whatever he does shall prosper" (Psalm 1:1-3).

God has provided a river—an abundant supply of grace that flows from His throne. It flows from His place of authority to empower our lives for His purposes. This river brings blessing, joy, and life wherever it moves. In His grace, we find energy, vision, provision, perseverance, and everything we need to fulfill His call.

Thank you, Jesus, for this abundant supply of empowering grace!

Reflection Questions

How can you deepen your connection to the river of God's grace so that His life and healing flow through you to others?

How does the imagery of God's grace as a river change your understanding of the supply of God available to believers?

Abiding in the Vine: Living in the Life flow of Grace

In John 15, Jesus gives us another metaphor to describe our connection to Him. He compares it to a vine and its branches: "I am the vine, you are the branches. He who abides in Me, and I in him, bears much fruit; for without Me you can do nothing" (John 15:5).

The verses leading up to this show that fruitfulness is not something we are commanded to achieve on our own; it is a by-product of our connection to Jesus. He does not command the branches to bear fruit. Instead, the command is to abide in Him. The fruit comes naturally as a result of that connection.

In verse 6, Jesus warns that branches that do not abide in Him will be taken away and thrown into the fire. The warning is not about fruitlessness but about failing to remain connected to Him. Too many Christians live their lives barely connected to the life-giving flow of Christ.

Jesus desires that each person remains fully connected to Him as the Vine. The responsibility lies with us to stay connected.

The word abide means "to live, dwell, and remain." It speaks of an ongoing relationship with Him. Jesus makes it clear that we play a role in maintaining this connection. His warning is simple—stay connected.

This abiding relationship is part of God's grace to us. He has not simply saved us and left us to figure out life on our own. We are not expected to produce fruit in our own strength. His life and power flows through us, producing the fruit that glorifies the Father.

So how do we stay connected to this life-giving grace? By faith.

Faith is what connects us to the life flow of Jesus as our Vine. That life flow—the same grace that enables us to live out God's will—empowers us to bear fruit. When we abide in Jesus by faith, God's grace flows into and through our lives.

The writer of Hebrews tells us that faith is essential to pleasing God.

"But without faith it is impossible to please Him, for he who comes to God must believe that He is, and that He is a rewarder of those who diligently seek Him" (Hebrews 11:6).

In the original Greek, the phrase "without faith" does not just mean lacking faith—it implies being outside of faith. It describes faith as a place, like a building. A person can either be inside faith or outside of it.

This verse defines what it looks like to be "inside faith." It means coming to God, believing that He is present, and trusting that He rewards those who diligently seek Him.

When we come to Jesus in faith, believing that He is our Vine, we receive the reward of seeking Him. The rewards of God's lifeflow come as a byproduct of abiding in Him. Everything we need is in that flow of His grace.

We can either live as a branch connected to Jesus, receiving the lifeflow of grace, or we can disconnect and begin to wither. The things we attempt to do outside of faith do not please God.

This truth can be sobering when we realize that the same activity done at different times can have different spiritual outcomes. An action done in faith can please God, while the same action done outside of faith may not. This highlights the need to avoid a spiritual life that is merely about repetition, lifeless formulas and obligatory deeds. Instead, we are called to a vibrant, living relationship of active obedience with Christ.

Abiding in Jesus allows us to experience the life-flow of God's grace. Just as branches receive nutrients and life from the vine, we receive everything we need from Him. That flow of grace is what enables us to ultimately bear fruit.

If that connection is restricted, injured, or severed, we begin to wither and dry up. We may continue doing works, but they will lack the life of Jesus. They will be works done outside of faith, and will not be pleasing to God.

Staying connected to the Vine is not optional—it is essential. The grace of God flows through our relationship with Him, sustaining and empowering us to live fruitful, faith-filled lives.

Reflection Questions

How can you intentionally abide in a life-giving connection with Jesus to ensure His grace flows freely in and through you?

How can you actively cultivate a deeper sense of dependence on Jesus in both good times and difficult seasons?

CHAPTER FIVE

Accessing Grace

God's Grace Is His abundant supply

-Joseph Prince said. "The Lord told me once, 'Being under grace means being constantly under My supply. It means being conscious not of the need, demand, or crisis, but of My supply to you.'" [1]

God's grace is His constant, abundant supply. It is not a trickle. Consider what Paul writes about the overflowing abundance of God's grace:

"And God is able to make all grace abound toward you, that you, always having all sufficiency in all things, may have an abundance for every good work" (2 Corinthians 9:8).

Notice the words Paul uses to describe the level of abundance: "all grace," "abound," "all sufficiency," "in all things," and "abundance for every good work." This is not a picture of barely getting by. This is a powerful picture of Paul's inspired understanding of God's grace. It is a picture of overwhelming, superabundant grace. Think of Ezekiel's river, deep and overflowing, so vast it could not be crossed except by swimming.

In the same way, God's grace provides an abundance of energy, vision, supply, resources, faith, endurance, perseverance, and provision—everything that is needed.

A life connected to the abundance of God's grace does not mean the absence of challenge or trial. Consider the example of the apostles in the early church. They faced extreme hardships, yet God's grace equipped them to overcome extreme adversity. Paul writes to the church in Rome:

"Yet in all these things we are more than conquerors through Him who loved us" (Romans 8:37).

The phrase "more than conquerors" is translated from the Greek word *hupernikao*. Brian Simmons explains this term in the footnotes of The Passion Translation:

"The love of God gives us 'a glorious hyper-victory,' more than can be described or contained in one word. God's love and grace have made us hyper-conquerors, empowered to be unrivaled, more than a match for any foe!" (Romans 8:37 TPT).

Paul is saying that God's love is so powerful in believers' lives that they are over-equipped to handle any challenge they face. This should stir within us a desire to understand God's love and grace in a greater measure. Many times, life's challenges can feel overwhelming. But the truth remains—God's grace makes His people more than conquerors.

Looking at the context of Romans 8, the early church faced severe persecution, tribulation, distress, famine, nakedness, peril, and even death. Yet Paul still declared that they were, "more than conquerors." If they were over-qualified to handle such intense trials, how much more can God's grace empower us to navigate our own challenges?

This reminds us of Joseph in Genesis. When Jacob blessed his sons, he declared this over Joseph's life:

"Joseph is a fruitful vine, a fruitful vine near a spring, whose branches climb over a wall" (Genesis 49:22 NIV).

Joseph endured immense hardship—betrayal, slavery, false accusations, and imprisonment—yet he overcame each trial because of his connection to God. Jacob's declaration paints a powerful image: a vine may not be a towering tree, but it continues to grow no matter what stands in its way. If a rock lies in front of a vine, it climbs over it. If a wall blocks its path, the vine grows higher than the wall. No matter the obstacle, the vine finds a way to overcome and rise to the occasion.

Paul's life reflected this same principle. He was shipwrecked, beaten, imprisoned, left for dead, and faced hunger and suffering. Yet, through grace, he endured and fulfilled God's call. His example reveals how grace empowers believers to persevere.

This truth applies to every believer. Trusting in the all-sufficient supply of God's grace allows us to overcome any challenge that He calls us to face. Problems may seem insurmountable, but His grace empowers us to rise above them as we depend on the Lord.

Reflection Questions

How does the imagery of Joseph's vine and Paul's endurance encourage you in difficult seasons?

What practical steps can you take to deepen your reliance on God's grace in everyday life?

Sufficient Grace

The apostle Paul goes even further in his letter to the Corinthian church to describe his "thorn in the flesh." When he pleaded with God to take it away, this was God's response:

"And He said to me, 'My grace is sufficient for you, for My strength is made perfect in weakness.' Therefore most gladly I will rather boast in my infirmities, that the power of Christ may rest upon me. Therefore I take pleasure in infirmities, in reproaches, in needs, in persecutions, in distresses, for Christ's sake. For when I am weak, then I am strong" (2 Corinthians 12:9-10).

Paul reveals that weakness actually magnifies the grace of God. One preacher suggested that Samson may not have been a massive, muscular figure like the caricatures often depict. If Samson had been built like Goliath, the Philistines might have assumed his strength came from his own physique. Instead, it was clear that his power came from the Lord.

Imagine witnessing a professional weight lifter walk into a grocery store parking lot, bend down, and pick up a car to move it out of the way. Everyone watching would marvel at his strength, exclaiming, "Wow! Did you see how strong that guy is?" But now imagine a thin, petite woman doing the same thing. Instead of commenting on her physical strength, people would demand to know, "How did she do that?!" There would have to be another explanation beyond her own ability.

This is the reality of how God works through His people. The life and power of Jesus is what empowers us. When an ordinary person accomplishes something extraordinary, God gets the glory! Paul was making this point to the Corinthian church—he actually rejoiced in his weaknesses so that no one could mistake the source of his strength. His life became undeniable evidence of God's power at work. If God could do it for Paul, He can do it for anyone!

Sometimes, people assume pastors and ministers must be different from others because of the miraculous testimonies surrounding their lives. But all those who God uses are simply normal people who love Jesus. Ministers who try to put on airs or act like they have some special status only diminish God's glory by trying to increase their own. The more average and normal a person appears, the more obvious it is that God is the one working through him or her. Many would be surprised at how utterly dependent some of the most effective ministers are on the Holy Spirit—even for simple things like remembering names, planning details, or overcoming personal insecurities and intimidation. The secret to their success is total reliance on God.

This is seen in the story of Gideon. God commanded him to reduce his army to just three hundred warriors for one reason—so that the victory would clearly be credited to God. He specializes in taking ordinary people and using them as vessels for His glory!

For this reason, we must never allow circumstances, the enemy, or even the great testimonies of others to diminish the value of our own walk with God. Walking in simple obedience to His Word and following the prompting of the Holy Spirit puts us on the front lines of seeing God move in powerful ways.

God did not allow Paul to use his "thorn in the flesh" as an excuse to step back from ministry or be disobedient. Instead, He supplied Paul with overcoming grace to continue, despite the challenges. Likewise, His grace is more than enough for us to fulfill His call, no matter what obstacles we face.

Reflection Questions

Have you ever experienced God using you in spite of any of your weaknesses or inabilities?

Is there any area in which you are too intimidated to step out in faith? Are you ready to submit that area of your life to God?

Here for All

Abundant grace of God is available to everyone! John writes: "And of His fullness we have all received, and grace for grace" (John 1:16).

Some theologians refer to this as "common grace." However, in my view, calling anything from God "common" does not seem fitting. A better way to describe it might be "universal" or "freely dispersed grace," as God's grace is available to all who respond. Every person has the grace from God to receive grace from God. Every person has the ability to recognize truth when they hear it. Even before being born again, God places within every heart the capacity to perceive and respond to His universal grace.

Paul urges the Corinthian believers not to squander the provision God had made for them in Christ:

"We then, as workers together with Him also plead with you not to receive the grace of God in vain" (2 Corinthians 6:1).

The Corinthian church had received the gospel through Paul, yet they had begun to fall into ungodly behaviors. In concern, Paul pleads with them not to receive God's empowering grace in vain.

What does this mean? This message is just as relevant today. There is an abundant supply from God meant to be received, lived in, and expressed. Grace is not something to be ignored or set aside. Just as someone might hear the gospel and choose not to respond, a believer can also hear about the abundant, empowering grace available to them and do nothing with it.

In the next chapter, we will explore how to receive and walk in the empowering grace of God. Heed Paul's plea—do not receive God's grace in vain. Do not simply hear about it, shrug it off, and move on. Engage with it, apply faith to it, and explore the depths of what God has for you. Grow in the grace of God, for the fulfillment of His purpose in your life depends on it.

Reflection Questions

How can believers ensure they are not receiving God's grace in vain?

Are there any scenarios in your relationships with others, where you recognize a greater dependency on God's grace is needed?

ENDNOTES
1. https://www.josephprince.com/meditate-devo/grace-that-supplies Faith and Grace

CHAPTER SIX

Faith and Grace

Grace in Everyday Life

The more I experience God's empowering grace, the more I have come to rely on it as essential. As I lived this out in my everyday life, my expectation began to grow regarding how much grace could impact my day to day life. I have even experienced the grace of God flow to my life in situations that don't seem very "spiritual" at all! A defining moment brought this understanding into focus.

While serving as a missionary in another nation, several complex challenges arose concerning international banking and real estate law. Our residency status was changing, and navigating the legal and financial processes in a foreign country seemed overwhelming. Any misstep could result in frozen accounts and would have significant financial implications to our finances. We needed international banking and investment advice that fit our unique situation. With only two days to resolve everything before a scheduled flight out of the country, I lifted up a simple prayer. "God help me, I don't know what I don't know. The decisions that I am making today will have lasting implications. I need you to Father me through someone here at this bank today." As I was ushered towards an extremely long and slow-moving line, a man carrying a large stack of papers stepped in line in front of me. A lighthearted joke about being stuck behind him with his big stack of papers sparked a conversation.

Hearing my accent, he inquired about my background and work. I mentioned how I was a minister, and was open about the situation and that I was there today because I needed specific guidance on real estate and international banking. He chuckled and responded, "I usually send my employees to the bank, but today I had to come in person. I own a firm that specializes in exactly that."

As we waited together in that long line, he patiently explained every detail, providing a clear road map for the entire process we would need to take. By the time I reached the bank counter, every question was answered. Our attempts to find this man later to express gratitude were unsuccessful. In that moment, God's grace and provision were undeniable. His perfect supply was provided at the perfect time.

God's grace is available to all. He resources His people, not only through spiritual encounters but also through everyday interactions. His provision often comes in unexpected ways, and being able to recognize it deepens our trust in God's guiding hand in our lives.

Reflection Questions

In what ways have you experienced God's unexpected provision in your own life?

How can you develop a greater awareness of God's grace working in your daily challenges?

What steps can you take to trust God more fully in uncertain or overwhelming situations?

Accessing God's Grace

How do we connect to this amazing and constant supply of God's grace? The answer is clear. It is the same as when we first come to Him. We receive His grace by faith the moment we surrender our lives to Jesus.

"And He raised us up together and made us sit in heavenly places in Christ Jesus, that in the ages to come He might show the exceeding riches of His grace in His kindness towards us in Christ. For by grace you have been saved through faith" (Ephesians 2:6-8).

We receive God's grace through faith. "And that not of yourselves; it is the gift of God." While this verse specifically speaks of salvation, it is just the beginning of our experience of God's grace. The same faith that brings salvation continues to give us access to the supply of God's grace in every area of life.

Another scripture reinforces this truth:

"Through whom we have access by faith into this grace in which we stand and rejoice in the hope of the glory of God" (Romans 5:2).

Supernatural encounters with God are simply manifestations of His grace. To Him, they are completely natural. It is His power, His ability, His orchestration, and His gifts of the Holy Spirit at work. All of these things are accessed by faith.

Paul explains how faith interacts with God's gifts and power, specifically in the area of prophecy:

"Having then gifts differing according to the grace that is given to us, let us use them. If prophecy, let us prophesy in proportion to our faith" (Romans 12:6).

This verse reveals an important connection between faith and the manifestation of God's power. Faith determines the extent to which God's gifts operate in our lives. Some people believe they have only one specific gift of the Spirit from 1 Corinthians 12 while lacking others. However, this is a misunderstanding of how the gifts of the Spirit function. The word "gifts" is not the most accurate English translation. A better translation is "manifestations." The gifts of the Holy Spirit are manifestations of the Spirit Himself. This means that anyone filled with the Holy Spirit has the potential for all nine manifestations to operate in their life. The Holy Spirit decides how and when He moves through us as we engage our faith.

Paul states in Romans 12:6 that faith plays a significant role. Many who say they have the gift of healing, but not the gift of prophecy, often simply lack the faith for the Holy Spirit to use them in this way. They are not limited by God, but by their own faith. As faith grows, so does the experience of God's grace! It is not that His grace is lacking. It is that our faith must develop so that we can access His grace more fully.

I am not suggesting that people should try to make something happen that the Holy Spirit is not directing them to do. But, a lack of faith can restrict the flow of God's grace and hinder the operation of the Holy Spirit's manifestations in our lives. We need to engage with God's Word about how these gifts of the Spirit are used so that our faith grows and we can start to function as the Holy Spirit leads us.

In a future chapter, we will explore more about how God's grace works personally and individually in our lives. But for now, the key takeaway is this. Faith is how we access the work of God's grace. The more we grow in faith, the more we experience the abundant manifestations of His Spirit at work in our lives.

Reflection Questions

How does viewing spiritual gifts as "manifestations" rather than fixed abilities impact your expectations of how God can use you?

What practical steps can you take to increase your faith?

Strengthening Faith by Remembering God's Faithfulness

There is so much more to experience in God. As our faith rises and is exercised, the flow of grace to our lives will become evident through the manifestation of His Spirit! This may sound simplistic to some, while to others it might bring to mind the excesses of the "Word of Faith" movement, where people were accused of being "name it and claim it" or "blab it and grab it" Christians. However, just because some have tried to misuse faith for personal gain does not mean we should ignore its true power. The prevalence of a counterfeit one hundred dollar bill does not negate the fact that real ones exist. In the same way, the truth is that faith must be applied according to the Word of God and the guidance of the Holy Spirit in every area of life.

When faith is lacking, it becomes difficult to see the grace of God at work. Thoughts and emotions can begin to align more with defeat and discouragement. Has God's grace changed? No. It is still flowing all around, just like a river. The difference is that faith has weakened, making it harder to connect with His grace as before. The good news is that this disconnection is reversible.

King David experienced this in his life. When he felt discouraged, he strengthened himself by remembering what God had done in the past.

During a particular season of travel, I faced intense intimidation in a specific region. The spiritual warfare was so strong that I struggled to even remember my own testimonies of God's power that I had witnessed. To counteract this, I literally started writing down a list of miracles I had personally witnessed. This helped me recall God's faithfulness even when I felt overwhelmed.

Many Psalms reveal this pattern in David's life. He often begins by pouring out his heart, expressing deep distress and feelings of abandonment. Then, halfway through the psalm, his perspective starts to shift and we start to hear something similar to this: "And then I remembered the goodness of the Lord. I remembered all that He has done. In fact, those memories start to consume my thoughts, and I cannot forget them." Psalm 77 is a great example of this transformation.

God's testimonies and faithfulness never changed, but David's focus did. He moved from a place of doubt to a place of faith, trusting in what God was going to do. This is how faith works in our lives today. Faith in God's grace allows us to step into the ongoing work of the Holy Spirit's transformation. As we walk in relationship with Him, abiding in Him as our vine (John 15), we receive His grace through faith.

Reflection Questions

How have you experienced God's faithfulness in difficult times in your life?

What regular practices help you remember and bring to mind the truth and goodness of God in your life?

Grow in Faith for Grace

In order to experience more of the grace of God in our lives, we need to grow our faith. Faith is like a wire that connects us to the supply circuit of God's works. Recognizing this, the disciples asked Jesus to increase their faith as recorded in Luke 17:5, "And the apostles said to the Lord, 'Increase our faith.'"

This request came in the context of forgiving someone who repeatedly sinned against them. The high standard Jesus set challenged their faith. They understood the emotional toll of extending limitless forgiveness. Acknowledging their need, they asked for greater faith so that they would be able to meet this standard.

Many believers face situations that seem beyond their current level of faith. It is one thing to know that God's grace is sufficient, but another to maintain unwavering faith in that truth. There are seasons when faith wavers, making it difficult to remain connected to the flow of God's grace.

One of those seasons for me was from mid-2020 to 2021. While the world was dealing with COVID-19, there would come additional challenges in my life for which I would need to rely on God's grace and strength beyond my own capacity.

I was four months into my new role as the lead pastor at our church when the pandemic hit. Pastoring in that season was uniquely difficult, with people deeply polarized, scared, and angry. Despite the turbulence of the times, God gave us a unique strategy that led to church growth. Yet the pressure remained intense.

In June of that year, we were blessed to purchase our dream home through an auction. Two weeks after putting down a significant deposit, the purchase was suddenly in jeopardy. A situation on our neighbor's property threatened the sale of our existing home.

Over the next several months, we were stretched to the limit. The new house required major renovations before it could accommodate our family. The old house, which we now could not sell, needed extensive work. That year I worked full-time pastoring then spent my evenings and nights doing construction. Hiring professionals was not an option due to our financial constraints. We were juggling zoning regulations, legal matters and building inspectors for both properties simultaneously, as well as dealing with banks all while balancing church leadership in a tough season.

One Sunday morning before preaching, I received a message that one of our buildings had a fire and the fire department was called and put it out. Assuming it was minor because the person did not bother to call but text, I preached during the service before following up. It turned out to be a significant fire, leading to a major insurance claim. By God's grace, no one was hurt, but this added another massive project to an already complex season.

After four months of consistent labor, our family moved into the newly acquired house, even though things were not entirely finished. With that move, renovations on the old house began in earnest. Our finances were nearly depleted. Completing the needed work seemed impossible. Unexpectedly, the insurance payout from the fire arrived at a critical time, helping us stay financially afloat. Several church members, family, and friends stepped in with their labor and expertise, providing much-needed support.

Amidst all this, one of our family members was in a serious car accident that totaled the vehicle. By God's protection, everyone who was involved was unharmed. Once again, the insurance payout arrived just when we needed to cover major expenses. We saw firsthand the truth of Romans 8:28. What the enemy meant for evil, God turned for good.

Just as we thought things could not get any more difficult, they did. A buyer really wanted to purchase our mission home that we owned in another country. We started the process and then suddenly the deal unexpectedly fell through. Over the next weeks, multiple buyers backed out due to the economic downturn caused by COVID-19. Then we learned that documents from the previous homeowners were missing in the local government. They had built an addition onto the house years before we bought it. But the local government lost the architectural plans and this created an issue. In order to sell, we needed to obtain "as-built" architectural plans, submit them for approval, and pass inspections—as if the addition in this home had just been built–even though it had been fifteen years since the previous home owners had added the addition.

For months, I woke up in the early morning to handle all the communication details of the architects, inspectors and real estate agents from a different time zone overseas, then worked a full day at church, came home to eat quickly and spent my nights doing renovations. Exhaustion set in while the responsibilities kept piling up.

During this time, I was asked to consider stepping into the role of International Director for DOVE International. It was an honor. Yet, being asked to be the successor of a founder who led a worldwide ministry for over forty years added many more complex meetings and changing dynamics to an already strenuous season. We knew it was God, but it felt like this could not have come at a more stressful time for us.

As if all of this was not enough, tragedy struck when our real estate agent overseas and his wife both suddenly passed away from COVID-19. No one at their real estate office knew where our house keys were or the status of the various inspections that they were managing on our behalf. The country was in lockdown, making it impossible to travel there. Emotionally and physically, an army of challenges was pressing in from all sides.

Through all of this, God kept telling me it would be okay. He assured me that we were going to make it. The weight of ongoing financial, emotional, and logistical battles was taxing. The pace of life seemed to be beyond reason. When people asked how we were doing, I often lacked the words to explain. Much of what we were facing was not public knowledge, and even when I tried to describe it, people just stared in disbelief. Eventually, I stopped explaining and simply asked for prayer. And people prayed.

In that season, my faith was stretched beyond anything I had previously experienced. Through it all, God's grace sustained us. He provided when we thought there was no way forward. So many miracles came together as God wrapped up that intense season in our lives. A whole book could be written about God's faithfulness in that twelve month period of our lives. He sent people to help at just the right moments. We experienced miracles of provision and strength that, to this day, are hard to wrap our heads around. Even in the darkest moments, He reminded us that He was still in control.

Faith is what connects us to the flow of God's grace. When challenges increase, faith must grow to match them. Looking back, I see how God used that season to expand my faith in ways I never imagined. God is so faithful and so good, even in the hardest times.

Reflection Questions

Have you ever had your faith tested?

Have you experienced the presence of God with you while in the fire of trial? How did He walk you through?

Grace in Hardship

I do not think we would have made it without our family, friends, and mentors who gathered around us in that twelve-month window of time. My strength was flagging. My wife and children were along for this crazy ride, and as much as possible, we worked on these projects together. We simply committed ourselves to keep going and not stop, trusting God to get us through. Any given week of that period, I was at max stress and running close to exhaustion.

I was continuing to lead the church through COVID while also navigating the significant transition of becoming the lead pastor. This meant onboarding key new staff roles and supporting others overseas as they walked through pressure and trials as COVID 19 impacted their own country. At the same time we were stepping into a significant succession process at an international level. I was preaching, praying with people, listening to their challenges, and visiting them when they needed it.

Even though emotionally I could hardly believe the compounding effect of everything we were walking through, I encountered a strength and a peace that was not my own. My own strength could only bring me to stand up in the mornings, but God's grace carried us and continued to minister through us. After twelve months, things slowly began to be resolved, and we were finally able to finalize some of these demanding projects. At last, we could start the long road to financial and emotional recovery.

Even though our inner capacities were stretched to the extreme, we witnessed many miracles during this time. We experienced miraculous financial provision, often arriving at just the right moment. Unexpected delays in major bills and work timelines worked together in ways that we still do not fully understand. Every time a major bill needed to be paid, we somehow had just enough to cover it. It was nothing short of miraculous!

As a family, we would not have made it without one another. Even as I write this years later, I still feel a slight tightness in my chest remembering that incredibly intense season. We would not have made it through without God's voice being near and Him walking with us daily. We would not have made it without those who prayed for us and the family and friends who stepped in to help. We are forever grateful for God's faithfulness.

Some people equate walking in faith with the absence of challenges, but that is simply not true. When we look at Scripture, we see that hardships are normal. Many times, people come to the end of their own strength, and it is only God's grace and their faith in Him that sustains them. One thing I know for certain is that we would not have survived that season without God's grace. There are others who have gone through much worse, and my heart goes out to them. I know that God's grace is available for them as well. During this same period of time we knew many people who were experiencing deep places of grief and tests of their own faith.

Seasons of hardship come with great personal cost. Yet God holds us together. Hebrews 4:16 describes the type of help we receive from the throne of grace:

"Let us therefore come boldly to the throne of grace, that we may obtain mercy and find grace to help in time of need" (Hebrews 4:16).

The word "help" here in Greek refers to the process of frapping a ship. During strong storms a wooden vessel could easily break apart, so the crew would pass ropes or chains under the ship and secure them tightly. This reinforcement literally held the ship together and strengthened it to survive the rough seas. This is exactly the type of help that we can count on from the Lord in challenging times. God's help holds us together in the rough seas of life.

God's grace was in abundant supply over that twelve-month period, but our faith also had to rise in order to receive of His grace. Giving up would have caused everything to collapse around us.

The Bible compares us to earthen vessels in 2 Corinthians 4:7: "But we have this treasure in earthen vessels, that the excellence of the power may be of God and not of us."

As earthen vessels, our role is to be present with the Lord and be obedient to God's instructions so that His glory and miraculous work can shine through. Our job is to stay in a place of faith and obedience, trusting that His strength will carry us, even in the most difficult challenges.

Reflection Questions

In what ways did you discover God's help, even if your own strength was faltering?

How does the imagery of "frapping a ship" deepen your understanding of God's sustaining grace during times of extreme pressure?

Growing in Faith

As we grow in our faith, we are simply increasing our ability to receive more of what is already available to us in God's grace.

"But you, beloved, building yourselves up on your most holy faith, praying in the Holy Spirit" (Jude 1:20).

Jude tells us that one way to build up our faith is by praying in the Holy Spirit. Spirit-led prayer and praying in tongues strengthens and edifies faith, helping believers connect more deeply to the grace of God.

Praying in tongues has been an essential part of my Christian walk. When I pray in tongues my faith is strengthened. This practice of dependence on the Holy Spirit is essential. There is no reason to hesitate in displaying our dependency on the Lord through prayer.

The Bible makes a clear distinction between praying in tongues as a personal prayer language, which builds up faith, and speaking a message in tongues to the church, which requires interpretation. Some misunderstand this difference and criticize those who pray in tongues aloud, believing that if it is not followed by interpretation, that people should remain silent. In most churches that believe this, nobody ever speaks in tongues. Yet the early church relied heavily upon the Holy Spirit in this way.

Paul clarifies this in 1 Corinthians 14:14, "For if I pray in a tongue, my spirit prays, but my understanding is unfruitful."

Paul also instructs in 1 Corinthians 14:39 that believers should never forbid speaking in tongues. The prayer language of tongues is direct communication between a believer's spirit and God. It is a supernatural way to bypass the limitations of human reasoning and align with the Holy Spirit's guidance.

When facing situations that require strong faith, the rational mind may not be helpful. In fact, it can sabotage what God wants to do. Fear, doubt, and confusion can cloud our thinking. In those moments, praying in the Spirit allows faith to rise above emotions.

When people seek ministry and prayer, they often recount their problems in great detail. While sharing concerns is natural, an overemphasis on circumstances can reinforce fear, worry, and hopelessness. This is not to say that honesty is wrong, some even go to the extreme of distorting the truth of their circumstances in the name of positive confession. However, when seeking prayer for divine intervention for healing, encouragement, or breakthrough, allow the focus to be on what you are asking from the Lord. You may not need to go into every detail of the difficulty or the diagnosis. What is truly needed in those moments is beyond human reasoning.

Praying in tongues builds us up. This kind of prayer shifts our focus from fear to faith and from uncertainty to divine courage. Once faith is built up, challenges can be approached with a victorious mindset of the finished work of Jesus on the cross rather than from a place of struggle.

Paul was deeply aware of this benefit and practiced it often, as he states in 1 Corinthians 14:18 "I thank my God I speak with tongues more than you all."

Because praying in tongues builds up faith, and faith is how God's grace is accessed, the practice of praying in tongues is a powerful tool for walking in greater fullness of what He has made available to us in His grace. The supply of His grace is constant; believers simply need to stay connected to it.

Reflection Questions

How does praying in tongues help strengthen faith and connect believers to God's grace?

How can you incorporate praying in the Holy Spirit more consistently in your daily walk with God?

CHAPTER SEVEN

Growing in Grace

Growing in the Holy Spirit

Because God's grace is super abundant, the journey to understanding how to experience more of it is ongoing. We can intentionally aim our faith and expectation to receive more from God.

There was a time in my life when the supernatural gifts of the Holy Spirit were not part of my experience. Coming from a blue-collar background in the agricultural industry, the move of the Holy Spirit was new to me and my family. However, a move of God was stirring in the region during my childhood and several churches were experiencing revival. It became common to see people respond to altar calls for prayer and ministry. As a boy, I felt a deep hunger for God.

As I was growing up, my local church was essentially a gymnasium with a stage, but the presence of the Lord was there. I would frequently respond to altar calls and receive ministry. Seeing people fall down under the power of God was common, and these encounters became personal as well.

One night in our youth group meeting, leaders were praying for those seeking a fresh filling of the Holy Spirit. Having already received a prayer language from the Lord a few years earlier, I still hungered for more of God. I was around the age of thirteen years old and responded to an invitation to receive prayer. The presence of God washed over me with overwhelming waves until I lost my balance and fell down under the power of God. Laying there, with wave after wave of His presence cascading through me, my life was forever changed.

They told me later that I had taken out several rows of chairs as I had fallen in the Holy Spirit. The next awareness I had was of lying on the floor, filled with the tangible love and power of God. I had no pain from this experience, no memory of hitting the ground, just the undeniable encounter with His presence. It was a time in the church when many were experiencing similar moves of God.

Even after this power encounter with the Lord, I did not personally experience the gifts of God flowing through my life to others until later. I learned this through spending time with those who were actively walking in the gifts of the Holy Spirit in their own life. Time spent with evangelists, prophets, and those who had faith for healing dramatically impacted my view of what was possible! What had changed? My knowledge, faith, and experiences were growing together. Much of my growth happened in Bible college, where the environment nurtured a belief that God desires to empower His people with signs, wonders, and miracles. This is not for the sake of making us look good, but for the sake of empowering His people with a divine advantage to accomplish His will.

Bible college became a greenhouse for spiritual growth. Being surrounded by other young men and women who were passionately pursuing God created an atmosphere of expectation. Lectures focused on studying God's Word, drawing a straight line through Scripture from Genesis to Revelation on specific topics, and learning how He used leaders both in the past and present. This setting cultivated faith rather than suppressing it. One key exercise required of the students was personally summarizing each chapter of the Bible. This reinforced an understanding of how God interacts with His people. As faith and knowledge grew together, the power and gifts of the Holy Spirit began manifesting in my life in new and tangible ways.

You may not be in a season where you can go to Bible college, but each one of us can receive from the Lord in our own way. We often do this through connecting with a church and community of believers. Ask the Lord to help you grow in utilizing the gifts of the Holy Spirit. Actively seek out relationships with those who display the evidence of the gifts of the Holy Spirit. Ask the Lord to bring people who can mentor and teach you.

"So I say to you, ask, and it will be given to you; seek, and you will find; knock, and it will be opened to you. For everyone who asks receives, and he who seeks finds, and to him who knocks it will be opened. If a son asks for bread from any father among you, will he give him a stone? Or if he asks for a fish, will he give him a serpent instead of a fish? Or if he asks for an egg, will he offer him a scorpion? If you then, being evil, know how to give good gifts to your children, how much more will your heavenly Father give the Holy Spirit to those who ask Him!" (Luke 11:9-13)

Reflection Questions

How has surrounding yourself with Spirit-filled believers helped you grow in the gifts of the Holy Spirit?

What steps can you take today to ask, seek, and knock for a deeper experience of the Holy Spirit?

Increase our Faith

Another way faith increases in our hearts is when we truly hear and respond to God's Word. Paul told the church in Rome: "So then faith comes by hearing, and hearing by the word of God" (Romans 10:17).

Our ability to receive increases as we apply this principle. Paul does not merely state that faith comes by hearing God's Word; he emphasizes that hearing itself is produced by the Word of God. This unique phrasing holds significant meaning.

Deuteronomy 6:4-5 states: "Hear, O Israel: The LORD our God, the LORD is one! You shall love the LORD your God with all your heart, with all your soul, and with all your strength."

The Hebrew word *shama* means more than simply perceiving sound; it implies truly listening, taking heed, and responding with obedience. When God commanded Israel to "hear," He was calling them to internalize His words and allow them to shape their lives. However, what precedes the greatest commandment in these verses is often overlooked. We are not only instructed to hear, but also to respond appropriately, as a by-product of what we have heard.

Verse five of Deuteronomy 6 introduces the greatest commandment. God was instructing Israel to first "hear," listening with an openness that would allow His words to immediately and totally impact their lives. They were to receive and be transformed by what came next: the command to love the Lord with all their being. This command was meant to revolutionize their daily lives and influence every part of their existence.

Looking at the broader context of Romans 10, Paul is addressing Israel's response to the gospel. Though they heard the message, they did not obey it. Multiple times in this chapter, he points out their disobedience. Their testimony was not one of faith but of resistance, because they failed to truly listen and respond.

To put it another way, faith comes by being open to learning, being willing to be impacted by what we hear, and being eager to respond appropriately. It requires active listening with the intent of heeding. However, we cannot simply absorb everything we hear! This is where the second part of Romans 10:17 becomes crucial. The Word of God serves as the filter, teaching us what we should or should not allow to enter in and impact our lives.

In today's world, many narratives compete for attention on the news, social media, and campuses. Movements and counter movements constantly trend online. Unfortunately, well-intended people sometimes get caught up in misguided ideas. How do we discern what we are to listen to? How do we sharpen our ability to hear so we are not gullible, swayed by every compelling argument and idea?

The word of God is our standard of truth. It trains us to hear, heed, and respond appropriately. By examining the cause and effect relationship in Romans 10:17, we see that active engagement with God's word enhances our ability to discern truth. Faith grows when we listen with the intention to obey and be changed by the truth of God that we hear. Faith comes by hearing. But true, discerning, and transformative hearing comes by the word of God. It is through scripture that we learn to recognize and embrace truth, allowing it to shape our lives.

Reflection Questions

In what ways can you develop a habit of listening to God with the intent to obey and be transformed?

How can you use Scripture as a filter to discern truth in a world full of competing narratives?

What practical steps can you take to ensure that your faith continues to grow through hearing God's word?

The Power of Active Faith: Hearing and Responding to God's Voice

Faith is not a one-time event based on something heard in the past, but an ongoing process of actively listening to God. Paul, in Romans 10:17, uses the present tense of "hearing," which means that faith grows as we continually engage with God's Word in our current circumstances.

The key idea is that faith is strengthened in the present moment when we actively listen to God's voice. When we clearly hear Him, we gain the guidance and confidence to navigate life's challenges.

Faith is not passive, but comes to those who have a heart that is open, attentive, and ready to respond to God's instruction. It flourishes when we have a living, ongoing relationship with God, where we consistently listen to His voice and align our lives with His guidance.

Jesus says in John 10:27 (NLT): "My sheep listen to my voice; I know them, and they follow me."

This is not the result of knowing a formula. In Mark 7:33, we read how Jesus used His own spit on a mute man's tongue to heal him. We only have a record of Jesus doing this one time. This does not mean that we should go around spitting on people when praying for healing. If the Holy Spirit directs us to do something "out of the ordinary," we need to be willing to do it. Rather the point is that people are often drawn to formulas. We can mistakenly think that because God worked in a particular way once, that He will work in the same way again and again.

It is God's intention that we be like the sheep that follow the voice of the Good Shepherd, relying on God's leading, unique to each situation, instead of practicing a "formula."

In the New Testament, we see several instances where Jesus and the apostles ministered to people in unique ways—often only once. In the Old Testament, God frequently changed Israel's battle strategies. At one time, Moses stood on the mountain with Aaron and Hur holding up his arms while Joshua led the army below. On another occasion, Joshua prayed for the sun and moon to stand still, and they did. Yet another time, the praise leaders and instrumentalists were sent ahead of the army.

These are not formulas to follow but examples of people who actively sought the Lord, listened to His voice, and obeyed His instruction. This is the model of active faith we are to follow today. These moments illustrate faith that comes when we are listening to the Lord while being deeply rooted in Scripture.

Reflection Questions

How can you develop a habit of continually listening to God in your daily life?

How can you balance being deeply rooted in Scripture while remaining sensitive to the Holy Spirit's direction?

Removing Barriers to God's Grace

God is the giver of grace. It is His work, a gift that cannot be earned. Yet, we receive His grace by faith. If we are passive and do not engage with God's grace through faith, we will miss the fullness of what He has made available to us.

God's grace is both a gift to receive and at the same time a reality to grow into. As we mature, we step into a greater experience of what He has provided. His grace is constantly at work in us and through us. To illustrate this, consider the metaphor of a lamp plugged in to a power source.

Recently, my wife wanted to use an antique-style lamp with an Edison bulb. However, the bulb was too bright, so we installed a dimmer switch to reduce the amount of electricity flowing to it. Thinking about the way dimmer switches work caused me to wonder if the enemy seeks to install dimmer switches in the lives of believers, diminishing the brightness of their light and limiting the flow of God's grace.

God's grace is like the electricity, available at full power in an outlet. A dimmer switch does not change the source of power but it does reduce its flow. Likewise, negative experiences, disappointments, pride, disobedience, or worldly distractions can act as dimmer switches, constricting faith and restricting the full expression of God's grace in our lives.

When faith is restricted, that restriction is like a dimmer switch that reducing our connection to God's grace. The enemy understands that if he can hinder the faith of believers, he can limit the impact of God's grace on the world through them. This is why we must actively resist anything that restricts our faith. Jesus likened believers to lamps that should not be hidden but placed where their light can shine brightly for all to see.

"Nor do they light a lamp and put it under a basket, but on a lampstand, and it gives light to all who are in the house. Let your light so shine before men, that they may see your good works and glorify your Father in heaven" (Matthew 5:15-16).

Jesus often addressed the disciples' lack of faith, not to shame them, but to reveal what was hindering God's power from flowing freely through their lives. The good news is that weak faith can be strengthened! By studying the Word of God, reflecting on His faithfulness, and responding to the Holy Spirit's leading, we strengthen our faith and access greater measures of the grace that is already available to us.

Reflection Questions

What "dimmer switches" in your life might be restricting the flow of God's grace, and how can you remove them?

In what ways can past disappointments or distractions hinder your connection to God?

Grace, Truth and Repentance

"For the law was given through Moses, but grace and truth came through Jesus Christ" (John 1:17).

Believers should watch that we don't fall into one of two ruts in our Christian walk.

One rut is embracing a sense of "truth" without grace. This often leads to harsh religious expressions, controlling environments, and legalism. In this rut, people position themselves as judges, enforcing strict rules meant to control others rather than lead them to Jesus. Conformity is demanded, and rigid interpretations of Scripture create extra-biblical guidelines that people must follow to remain accepted in their community. Repentance becomes a tool of control, and guilt and shame keep people trapped in insecurity and fear.

The other rut is embracing a watered down version of "grace", without truth. This mind-set distorts biblical grace into a worldly version that lacks a scriptural foundation. In this view, objective truth is dismissed. Faith becomes shallow, shaped by cultural norms and emotions rather than God's Word. This rut picks and chooses which Scriptures to accept while ignoring the rest. Repentance is rejected entirely, under the false assumption that God does not require His people to change.

Both of these extremes create religious systems that weaponize Scripture for their own purposes.

When we encounter the biblical Jesus, we experience both His grace and His truth. The balance of grace and truth keeps us from falling into these extremes and leads us into the fullness of God's will. This intersection of salvation, repentance, grace and truth is essential to our walk with Him.

Encountering the truth of Jesus requires us to take responsibility. True repentance and transformation demand honesty before God. Many people living in sin recognize their wrongdoing, but when they attempt to repent, they start justifying their actions. They deflect responsibility, blaming others for their choices, just as Adam did in Genesis 3 when he gave God the excuse that he had sinned because of the woman God had given him.

Yet, when we humble ourselves before God's truth and come to Him in genuine repentance, we are met with His grace. His grace does not condemn, but restores. It washes over us, setting us free and empowering us to live a changed life.

Peter experienced both the truth and grace of Jesus multiple times. In Luke 5:8, after witnessing the miraculous catch of fish, Peter was overwhelmed by Jesus' goodness and confessed his sinfulness. Yet, Jesus did not use Peter's awareness of his sin against him. Instead, He spoke words of grace, assuring Peter of his calling: "From now on, you will be a fisher of men."

Encountering the truth of Jesus can be raw and even painful, but it always leads to healing and restoration. At times, it may feel like open-heart surgery, but Jesus is the careful physician who uses a scalpel, not a machete. He does not merely treat symptoms—He gets to the root of sinful desires and brings true transformation. The process can be both gentle and painful, but it is always for our ultimate healing, not our punishment. He is the Great Surgeon, working deeply in our hearts to make us holy.

If we ignore His truth and refuse repentance, we hinder our own sanctification. When this happens, sin restricts the fruitfulness of God's grace in our lives. Embracing His truth means surrendering our own self-preservation and yielding to His Lordship. As we do, His grace changes us, making us clearer reflections of Him on the earth.

"But we all, with unveiled face, beholding as in a mirror the glory of the Lord, are being transformed into the same image from glory to glory, just as by the Spirit of the Lord" (2 Corinthians 3:18).

God promises to forgive freely all who come to Him. Grace does not just pardon. It transforms. Like the woman caught in adultery in John 8:11, whom Jesus forgave and instructed, "Go and sin no more," we are not left in a cycle of guilt or condemnation. The same grace that saves us also empowers us to live a life free from sin.

We do not live trying to earn forgiveness or make up for our past. Jesus has already paid the price for our freedom. When we allow His truth to do deep work in our hearts, His grace heals us at the core. He sets free from guilt and shame and empowers to walk victoriously. We will grow as we embrace both the truth and the amazing grace of God.

Reflection Questions

Are there areas in your life where you are still trying to earn forgiveness instead of fully receiving God's grace? How can you surrender those burdens to Him?

How can you actively embrace both God's truth and His grace in your daily walk, allowing Him to bring healing and freedom to your heart?

Humility and Faith: Keys to Greater Grace

Up until now, we have focused on the truth that God's grace is His abundant supply to each believer. What I am about to say does not contradict this. However, the Bible reveals a powerful way in which we can see the measure of God's grace increase in our lives. While an abundance is already available to us, there is a way to step into a greater level of grace, a superabundance if you will, diving deeper into the river of His grace.

The key to increasing the measure of grace in our lives is humility.

"But He gives more grace. Therefore He says: 'God resists the proud, but gives grace to the humble'" (James 4:6).

The Apostle James tells us that God resists the proud but gives grace to the humble. One way to experience more of God's work in our lives is through humility. This is a powerful truth!

Humility is a life posture that God actively seeks in His people. It is so important to Him that Scripture identifies it as the one clear way we can increase the amount of grace in our lives.

"Humble yourselves in the sight of the Lord, and He will lift you up" (James 4:10).

I once heard a preacher say that when we do our job of humbling ourselves, God does His job of lifting us up. However, if we try to do God's job and lift ourselves up, then He has to do our job of humbling us.

Can we take a moment and acknowledge that the right combination of faith and humility is beautiful? Many times, we see this beauty in older leaders who have weathered many storms and are finishing well. They have great faith and great humility. Some people focus so much on great faith that they lack humility, and eventually their arrogance becomes obvious. Others focus solely on humility but lack the boldness to accomplish great things for God. They sell themselves short because they are not willing to take any risks in faith.

It is a powerful thing when humility and faith are combined in an individual. This is the kind of leader Jesus was. It is a privilege to work with mature leaders who exhibit both humility and faith. Those who have walked with Jesus and have seen Him do amazing things often carry a perspective that is incredibly valuable to the body of Christ. When people have gone through the fire and come out not smelling like smoke, and when they have soared over the mountain tops with the Lord, there is a sweet, gentle strength about them.

"Likewise, you younger people, submit yourselves to your elders. Yes, all of you be submissive to one another and be clothed with humility, for 'God resists the proud, but gives grace to the humble'" (1 Peter 5:5).

Here, the Apostle Peter affirms that humility is the way to increase the measure of grace in our lives.

Humble faith is how we access greater measures of the grace of God. Faith plus humility. At times it can be confusing. The Lord spoke to my heart and said, "It can be a grave miscalculation to mistake faith for pride and apathy for humility." This caused me to ask: are there places where perceived humility is just a cover-up for apathy, or where great faith is mistaken as pride?

God desires deep and tender humility paired with lion-sized faith in His ability. Faith without humility can lead to arrogance, while humility without faith can lead to mediocrity. Great faith and great humility will increase our capacity to walk in great grace from the Lord.

Reflection Questions

In what ways have you seen faith and humility working together in your own life or in the lives of others? How can you cultivate both in your walk with God?

What steps can you take to grow in both humility and bold faith so that you can walk in a greater measure of God's grace?

Growing in Grace

The Apostle Peter gives a profound command in 2 Peter 3:18: "But grow in the grace and knowledge of our Lord and Savior Jesus Christ. To Him be the glory both now and forever. Amen."

Peter commands us to grow in God's grace. Just as we are called to grow in the knowledge of the Lord Jesus, we are also called to grow in grace. As discussed in previous chapters, there is no shortage of grace flowing toward believers from God. It is not that some have limited access to His grace while others receive it in abundance.

God's grace is like the river Ezekiel saw: a vast supply cascading toward every believer. However, that supply does not always manifest in our lives to the same measure, especially when our faith is small. Jesus often spoke to His disciples about their measure of faith because faith is essential to receiving more of God's grace.

Peter instructs us to grow in the grace of God. Grace is God's work, yet we can intentionally set our hearts and aim our faith to grow in His works. As our faith expands, we explore greater depths of His ever-flowing grace.

Sometimes God might come into our lives like a flood to wake us up to something special. But most of the time, we are the ones who will determine how deep in God we will go. We can remain ankle-deep, venture knee-deep, wade waist-deep, or fully immerse ourselves. Sometimes, God leads us deeper than we ever imagined, stretching us beyond our comfort. Like the difficult twelve-month period I previously shared, there are seasons when we rely entirely on His grace to carry us through each day. But there is also the choice to seek more, to grow in our ability to walk with God with our ears attuned to His heartbeat.

A helpful illustration comes from my son. One day, I saw him wearing some of my old clothes. They were baggy and too big for him. I know that one day he will become taller and stronger and grow into them, but at that moment, he still had some growing to do before the clothes would fit. The grace of God is similar. He gives it to us in generous portions, and as we mature in our relationship with Him, we grow into a deeper understanding of His ways. As we walk more closely with Him, we begin to fit into the spiritual "clothes" of grace that He has provided.

"He made known His ways to Moses, His acts to the children of Israel" (Psalm 103:7).

In the New Testament, each of us has the opportunity to walk closely with God, as Moses did, learning His ways rather than just witnessing His acts.

We must choose to obey Peter's command to grow in the grace of God. How do we do this? By growing our faith. I have heard preachers compare faith to a muscle—the more we exercise it, the more it grows. There is truth to this analogy. As our faith expands, more of God's grace flows and impacts our lives and those around us.

Reflection Questions

How does viewing grace as something we "grow into," like oversized clothes, change your perspective on spiritual maturity? Has your understanding of His grace deepened over time?

What practical steps can you take to move beyond witnessing God's acts to learning His ways? How can you intentionally exercise your faith so that it grows stronger?

Carriers of God's Grace

God's grace is meant to rest upon people, not systems or organizations. His plan is to release His grace into the earth through individuals who walk in His presence and power.

In 2 Samuel 6, the ark of the Covenant was outside of Jerusalem for over twenty years. During that time, the Israelites faced war with the Philistines. In a desperate attempt to secure victory, they brought the ark to the battlefield, assuming its presence would guarantee God's favor and victory.

But God's presence is no one's good luck charm! The Israelites treated His presence like a ritual object rather than honoring Him with true obedience. As a result, the Israelites were defeated and the Philistines captured the ark and kept it for seven months. However, after experiencing divine judgment, they quickly returned it.

The ark remained outside of Jerusalem for twenty years until David decided to bring it back. He organized a grand procession, placing the ark on a new cart pulled by oxen, accompanied by great rejoicing. But when the oxen stumbled, Uzzah reached out to steady the ark and was struck dead. The Bible says David became angry. Was it because God interrupted their celebration with judgement? Did David feel he deserved credit for having good intentions?

How often do we seek recognition for our good intentions rather than simply obeying God's instructions? At first David didn't understand, but after seeing how the house of Obed-Edom was blessed by the ark's presence, he realized God was teaching Israel a crucial lesson. They had lost the ark to the Philistines because they had presumed upon God's presence. Now, God was leading them away from that same presumption—the idea that they could control or manipulate Him or use Him for their own purposes.

God does not conform to human expectations. He alone sets the terms of His presence. When David grasped this, he changed his approach and humbled himself. The second time they transported the ark, he followed God's instructions: the Levites carried it on their shoulders, as God had commanded.

Good intentions are not a substitute for obedience to God's ways. Sincerity is not what God desires. David was sincerely wrong. There comes moments of surrender in the life of every believer where we will need to respond and lay down our sincere expectations on God and humble ourselves before Him.

Allowing Him to determine how He chooses to use our lives and our stories for His glory.

God's grace is not meant to rest on systems, formulas, or human-made structures. He chooses to place His grace upon people—those who carry His glory and reflect His light into the world. This is His plan for transforming society: His people, living out of obedience, shining like cities on a hill.

The role of leaders in the body of Christ is not to build large platforms or institutions. Their calling is to lead people into a deep encounter with God's grace and equip them to minister out of that grace to others. As believers encounter grace, they experience healing, freedom, and empowerment. This leads to mature, sustained victory over sin, and the ability to fulfill God's purpose in their lives for their generation.

Every believer carries a special portion from the Lord to bless and support others. In the next chapter, we will explore the specific roles individuals play in the community according to God's grace.

Reflection Questions

Are there any areas of your life where you might be relying on sincerity or good intentions instead of fully obeying God's ways? How can you surrender those areas to Him?

How have you seen God's grace at work through the lives of others around you? This week, make it a goal to write to one person about how their faith encourages you.

Great Grace

CHAPTER EIGHT

Specialized Grace

Impartation and Activation

There were times of training in my life where I received significant impartation from ministers and leaders who poured into me from their own deep experiences with God. I often experienced the greatest impact from those who had lived from the very principles they taught. Even today, I am constantly seeking to learn and glean from the experiences of others. I actively seek out input and counsel, recognizing the immense value this can have on my own life and faith journey. The people we surround ourselves with significantly help to shape our faith.

Although I regularly have opportunities to teach in many different environments, I still believe that the best training integrates theology along with boots-on-the-ground practical experience. This is essential for the growth and maturity of every believer. True equipping must go beyond intellectual understanding into practice. I have heard it said that some principles are caught more than they are taught. This is true. The best learning takes place when you can immediately go out and apply what you have just heard. ensuring that what you received becomes more than just head knowledge.

Each person carries a measure of God's grace specific to their calling and purpose. One team member I knew had a life motto that has stayed with me. She often challenged students to "run with the hungry," encouraging them to connect with those who passionately pursue the things of God. The people we surround ourselves with, and allow to shape our lives, will have a profound impact on our spiritual journey. When we see God moving in someone else's life, it strengthens our faith and broadens our expectations of how He can work in our own lives.

Reflection Questions

What steps can you take to actively seek out and learn from those who carry wisdom and experience?

In what ways can you ensure that your spiritual learning goes beyond knowledge and becomes practical experience?

How does witnessing God's work in others' lives expand your faith?

The Power behind Our Calling

When the Apostle Paul talks about the grace of God, it is clear that he has a specific and profound understanding of it. He does not merely refer to grace in general terms related to salvation. Instead, he speaks of grace as both power and authority from God to do certain things. Paul seems to refer to grace in a similar way to what we would call God's anointing.

One of the most striking verses about this is 1 Corinthians 15:10, where Paul says, "But by the grace of God, I am what I am, and His grace toward me was not in vain. But I labored more abundantly than they all, yet not I, but the grace of God which was with me."

Paul was not ministering out of his own strength or abilities. He recognized that another power was at work in him: God's grace. While he labored, it was ultimately God's grace working through him. His role in this labor was to be present, yielded, and responsive to God's direction. Just as Jesus only did what He saw the Father doing (John 5:19), Paul moved in unity with God. He kept pace with what God wanted to accomplish through him.

Up until now, we have primarily discussed God's grace in its universal availability to all, particularly in salvation, as it relates to our relationship with God, and eternity with Him. This remains absolutely true. Paul takes this concept even further by showing how God's grace applies uniquely to the specific calling, gifts, and assignments on an individual.

Paul sees grace as both universal and personal, tailored to the life and purpose God has for each believer. Galatians 2:9

specifically describes how Paul and Barnabas were received by the apostles in Jerusalem:

"When James, Cephas, and John, who seemed to be pillars, perceived the grace that had been given to me, they gave me and Barnabas the right hand of fellowship, that we should go to the Gentiles and they to the circumcised."

Paul and Barnabas were recognized as having a specific grace to preach to the Gentiles. According to what Paul writes in the book of Galatians, this grace was distinct from the grace given to the apostles in Jerusalem, whose primary mission was to preach to the Jews.

This grace for ministry among the Gentiles was tangible and evident. It was not just an internal calling, but something others could perceive. It was observable. The apostles in Jerusalem, who had initially been skeptical of Paul due to his past persecution of the church, now saw the undeniable grace of God upon his life. The very leaders of the church he once opposed and persecuted were now commissioning him into ministry leadership. What made the difference? The evident grace of God.

Reflection Questions

What does it mean for God's grace to be both universal and personally tailored to each believer's life?

In what ways can you recognize and cultivate the specific grace God has given you for your unique purpose?

Grace, Identity, and Calling

"But solid food belongs to those who are of full age, that is, those who by reason of use have their senses exercised to discern both good and evil" (Hebrews 5:14).

Hebrews 5:14 speaks about how our spiritual senses are sharpened through use. This shows us that we are not expected to instantly receive and know everything that we need to know. But by reason of using our spiritual senses, we are sharpened and we grow. God requires us to grow in discernment as we walk through life. Each person is on a journey of discovering the gifts and specific areas of grace that He has for them. His grace is both universal, applying to all, and uniquely tailored to each individual.

This concept is similar to the biblical principles of Christian marriage. The truths and principles found in God's word apply universally to all marriages. Principles such as forgiveness, overcoming and overlooking offense, treating a spouse with love and respect, selflessness, and mutual submission out of reverence for the Lord are foundational. When both spouses commit to these principles, marriage becomes a beautiful reflection of Christ and the church. These truths apply to every marriage, regardless of culture, background, or length of time married.

Yet every marriage is also unique. And the same foundational principles will be lived out in ways that are unique to each relationship. It is up to each couple to become students of one another, discovering how to apply these eternal truths in their specific relationship.

When my wife and I stood at the altar, I committed to becoming a lifelong student of her. No two marriages are exactly alike, just as no two snowflakes are identical, though all share the same essential properties. In marriage, couples embark on a journey of applying God's universal truths to the uniqueness of their own relationship.

This is also how the grace of God works. It is available and empowering for every believer yet uniquely suited to each person according to their calling. Paul writes in Ephesians 2:10 that there are "good works, which God prepared beforehand, that we should walk in them."

God gives each person a unique personality, set of desires, and talents. These are natural gifts from Him. The Apostle Peter affirms that every believer has received gifts from God's grace to serve others:

"As each one has received a gift, minister it to one another, as good stewards of the manifold grace of God" (1 Peter 4:10).

Each person has a purpose from God, but that purpose can only be fully realized through having a relationship with Him. Some may choose to live in a diminished measure of their calling. Natural abilities often shape the choices people make, even before they come to Christ. Many secular musicians, for example, have a God-given talent and passion for music but use it in ways that do not honor Him. In ministry travels, I have met successful business people who, despite their achievements, express a sense of emptiness, searching for deeper meaning in their success and life.

Specialized Grace

Without Christ, people experience only a partial version of who they were created to be. They may pursue God-given desires and talents and be widely successful, but without Christ, they still long for true purpose. When we come to Christ and are filled with the Holy Spirit, we are empowered to fully live out the purposes for which He created us. We receive specific gifts according to God's grace that we are meant to use, ministering them to others.

To a large extent, the study of personality types was often more accurately developed in secular fields then in the church. The world is continually searching for ways to increase effectiveness, productivity, and authenticity. Through observational science, many have attempted to decode personality traits and have made valuable discoveries. Unknowingly, they have simply identified aspects of God's intentional design coded into humanity.

However, this is only part of the picture. These insights reveal what can be known naturally, but in Christ there is so much more! While these studies may hold value, they do not bring salvation or spiritual life. Their real benefit is in helping believers understand how God has uniquely designed their personalities, motivations, and talents. He desires to rest His Spirit upon these natural attributes, supernaturally empowering them with His grace. Understanding the uniqueness of how God created each one of us allows us to be ready vessels of His grace, and prepared us to recognize the spiritual gifts that flow through us more effectively.

God places in each individual a unique and diverse combination of gifting and personal attributes, creating a beautiful display of His power and grace.

Reflection Questions

Why do you think natural abilities alone are not enough to bring true fulfillment? How does surrendering those gifts to Christ bring deeper meaning?

Take time to pray and ask the Holy Spirit to reveal areas where your talents, gifts, and calling align with His purpose. What do you sense Him highlighting?

Find your Sweet Spot in God's Grace

Each of us has desires, talents, personalities, and callings that were given to us by God. These combine to help us understand that there is more to be discovered and developed in life. The ultimate purpose of all of this uniqueness is to stir in us the desire to seek our Creator.

"So that they should seek the Lord, in the hope that they might grope for Him and find Him, though He is not far from each one of us" (Acts 17:27).

Consider how powerful life becomes when the intrinsic qualities God placed within us, our personality, talents, and desires, align with His empowering grace and the spiritual gifts given through the Holy Spirit. This alignment takes place in relationship with Christ and brings us toward the place of convergence. Convergence may be described as the state of operating in the fullness of the potential we are given from God.

The principle of convergence involves the intersection of several key factors: our natural talents, developed skills, personal history and experiences. God's calling, grace and gifting, financial resources, network of relationships, unique personality, and the opportunities before us. When these elements converge, they create a place of strength where we move forward with confidence and purpose. This will often contribute to seasons where there is great fruit and impact in our life.

The world defines success through wealth, influence, and power but God measures success differently. True success is Emmanuel, God with us. By the world's standards, the Apostle Paul did not appear successful, yet he fulfilled everything God called him to do, even going to Rome in chains to testify about Jesus.

Paul lived in such a way that God's grace consistently flowed through him to the churches. His letters continue to minister to us today. The same is true for the other apostles. John, for example, was imprisoned on the island of Patmos. Instead of succumbing to his circumstances, he wrote of powerful revelations of Jesus that still impact us. He remained faithful in God's grace even in difficulty. Eventually, he was freed and continued serving as an elder in the church of Ephesus until his death.

My friend Chris Smucker teaches about the difference between our comfort zone and our sweet spot. He says that God's grace brings us into our sweet spot, the place where we have the greatest effect with the least effort. Chris put it this way: "In baseball there is a small section of the bat that is called the sweet spot. When a player hits the ball with the sweet spot of the bat it will drive the ball significantly farther than hitting from any other place. The bat does not have to be swung extra hard but the fact that the ball hits the perfect spot on the bat sends it deep into the stands." Chris cautions us to understand that we are not to confuse the sweet spot with our comfort zone.

Our place of greatest convergence in God's will is often outside of what feels comfortable to our flesh. Many times, when we reach the end of our own ability, we encounter God's power and grace in new and profound ways.

From a natural perspective, Paul's sweet spot might have seemed to be ministering to the Jews. He was a Pharisee, the son of a Pharisee, trained under one of the most respected Jewish scholars of the day (Acts 22:3, 23:6, Philippians 3:5-6). He also had deep connections with the Jewish leadership in Jerusalem due to his history. Logically, it would have made sense for him to preach to the circumcised. Yet Paul ultimately realized that God's grace called him to preach to the Gentiles. This was his sweet spot; it was outside of his comfort zone.

Meanwhile, God sent Peter and John, former fishermen without formal religious training, to the Jews. Acts 4:13 says, "Now when they saw the boldness of Peter and John, and perceived that they were uneducated and untrained men, they marveled. And they realized that they had been with Jesus."

Their calling, like Paul's, required faith. It might have seemed natural for rough, miracle-working apostles from Galilee like Peter and John to relate better to the non-religious culture of Gentiles. Yet God called them outside of their comfort zones into the realm of faith in His grace. He often places us in situations where faith is required so that His grace can be revealed most powerfully. When we step beyond our own abilities, we find His life and power at work in us.

Reflection Questions

Write down moments in your life where you felt the greatest spiritual impact with the least effort. What patterns do you notice?

Paul's background naturally equipped him to minister to the Jews but he was called to the Gentiles instead. Have you ever felt called in a direction that seemed counterintuitive? How did you respond?

Grace and Sabbath

At times, something similar to what Paul describes in 1 Corinthians 15:10 happens when ministering to large groups of people. Recently, in Colombia, we began spontaneously ministering prophetically to each person in the room. Though the grace of God was still flowing, after hours of praying and prophesying, my body and emotions started to grow weary. Under the flow of grace you may not realize how tired you are becoming until later.

Maintaining physical and emotional health is essential to remaining strong so that God's grace can flow effectively. When the grace and anointing of God is moving, it may not be immediately apparent how tired the body is becoming. However, once the ministry moment passes, there is often the need for rest. This is why the principle of Sabbath is so important.

Although this is spoken from a ministry perspective, this truth applies to any area where God's grace empowers His people to accomplish extraordinary things in high-demand situations. The grace of God will continue to flow even when our bodies are reaching the end of our human capacity. In these moments, it is crucial to recognize the risk of coming close to physical or emotional exhaustion. Many powerful and anointed ministers have run themselves ragged, ministering under the anointing yet neglecting to care for their bodies and souls. When rest is ignored, vulnerability to poor judgment and burnout increases. The anointing and grace of God do not replace the need for Sabbath rest.

Regular Sabbaths are God's way of providing rest and renewal. Jesus said, "The Sabbath was made for man, not man for the Sabbath" (Mark 2:27). There may be seasons where the demands of life feel overwhelming. The greater the demands, the more intentional one must be in protecting times of rest with the Lord and family.

Sabbath is not just about withdrawing to sleep. It is a time to commune with the Lord in rest. Jesus modeled this beautifully. Scripture tells us that He often withdrew to quiet places to pray (Luke 5:16). In Matthew 13:1, Jesus simply sat by the lake. He prioritized time in stillness, enjoying communion with the Father and the Holy Spirit.

This oneness with the Father, Son, and Holy Spirit is what Jesus prayed for all believers in John 17:21. In this place of unity and rest, hearts and souls and bodies are renewed. Here, worship happens and we have the opportunity to receive from God and delight in His presence—not because we need to accomplish something, but to experience communion with Him.

The Old Testament command was to "Remember the Sabbath day and keep it holy" (Exodus 20:8). Notice that it does not say, "Remember the Sabbath day and keep it selfish." This is not just "me time." Personal time away is important, and incorporating recreation into the rhythms of life is valuable. However, the true Sabbath principle calls for time spent with the Lord of the Sabbath.

Prioritizing Sabbath rest with the Lord enables us to disengage from overly taxing situations and it also creates the capacity for us to be fully present later and enjoy times of recreation with family and friends. Without adequate times of Sabbath, disengaging from responsibilities can be a struggle. Sabbath is how we learn to release and trust the Lord with our responsibilities. Maintaining rhythms of rest and play in a busy schedule is an ongoing challenge, The Holy Spirit is present not only in the work He has called His people to do but also in moments of Sabbath, rest, and joy.

Building regular Sabbath intervals into life helps maintain the soul and body, ensuring that we are ready to be vessels for God's grace. We are responsible to steward ourselves well so that God's grace can work through us unhindered. As Paul describes in 1 Corinthians 15:10, the labor is to remain in a posture where His grace can work through His people to accomplish all He called them to do.

Reflection Questions

The Sabbath is not just about personal rest but about resting with the Lord. How does this perspective challenge or reshape your understanding of what it means to keep the Sabbath holy?

Jesus often withdrew to quiet places to pray. What are some practical ways you can follow His example in prioritizing stillness and communion with the Father in your daily or weekly routine?

In what ways do you experience the connection between Sabbath rest and your ability to be fully present with others in work, ministry, and recreation?

CHAPTER NINE

Trusting God's Grace

Grace Through One Another

God raises up people and gives them His grace to take on certain things. The famous revivalist John Wesley wrote to William Wilberforce, acknowledging that without God's empowerment, he would surely be exhausted by those determined to uphold slavery. However, Wesley believed that God gave Wilberforce a unique ability to bring an end to legalized slavery in England and urged him to persevere through every challenge he encountered, saying:

"Unless God has raised you up for this very thing, you will be worn out by the opposition of men and devils. But if God be for you, who can be against you? Are all of them stronger than God? O be not weary of well-doing! Go on, in the name of God and in the power of His might, till even American slavery (the vilest that ever saw the sun) shall vanish away before it." [1]

"According to the grace of God which was given to me, as a wise master builder I have laid the foundation, and another builds on it. But let each one take heed how he builds on it" (1 Corinthians 3:10).

It is important to recognize that just because something is hard does not mean there is no grace for it. Likewise, just because something is easy does not necessarily mean God's grace is present. If we could accomplish everything in our own strength, why would we need faith?

When God grants grace for a task or role, there is a supernatural element where things begin to work together in a significant way. By stepping into what He has called us to do, we learn to work with His grace, adapting for it and giving it preference. Over time, when our lives become oriented around how God's grace flows, we will recognize when God's grace is present.

Have you ever seen someone clearly operating in a grace-filled ability to serve God? Even in difficult circumstances, they are not striving in their own strength, yet they make challenging tasks look effortless. It is more than natural talent, charisma, or skill. It is a divine grace enabling them to accomplish what God has called them to do.

Titus 2:11-12 (TPT) says: "God's marvelous grace has manifested in person, bringing salvation for everyone. This same grace teaches us how to live each day as we turn our backs on ungodliness and indulgent lifestyles. And it equips us to live self-controlled, upright, godly lives in this present age."

Paul explains that not only did God's grace appear in person through Jesus, but the same grace that brings salvation also trains and equips us. This means that as we walk with Jesus, His grace continues to develop us.

As we grow in Christ, we learn to cooperate with God's grace. It is not something we either have or do not have; rather, it is something we grow in as we step into His calling for our lives. Over time, we become more specialized in the areas He has called us to, and spiritual gifts start to flow that further equip us for His work.

What is commonly referred to as the fivefold ministry gifts from Ephesians 4:11 are often called grace gifts. These are leadership gifts for the church. Jesus took the leadership that was upon His life and distributed it into five specific graces designed to equip His people for ministry, strengthen the body, and care for one another.

"But to each one of us grace was given according to the measure of Christ's gift" (Ephesians 4:7).

Verse 11 clarifies that these gifts include apostles, prophets, evangelists, pastors, and teachers. The purpose of these fivefold gifts is not to exalt individuals but to equip every believer.

God's ultimate goal is not merely powerful apostles, anointed prophets, dynamic evangelists, brilliant teachers, or compassionate pastors. His desire is for well-equipped saints. He wants believers to be apostolic, knowing how to build and expand His kingdom. He wants them to be prophetic, hearing His voice and loving His presence. He wants them to be evangelistic, sharing the gospel with those around them. He wants them to be grounded in His Word, instructed by teachers who love and impart truth. He wants them to have a shepherd's heart, caring for others with His love and compassion.

As believers are influenced by these fivefold ministry gifts, they grow in grace and become better equipped for ministry and serving one another. According to what we read in Ephesians 4:7, as the measure of Christ's gifts in a believer's life increases, the grace in his or her life also increases. There is a direct correlation. This might seem strange but we recognize this to be self-evident. When people attend churches that emphasize prophecy, they become more prophetic. The same is true when people attend a church that mainly emphasizes a teaching grace. They learn to come to each service ready to take good notes and become more teaching-oriented. When people are in a church that emphasizes pastoral ministry, they start to exude love, care and nurture for others.

Exposure to all five grace gifts edifies the body of Christ and leads to maturity. When each person functions in the measure of grace given to them, the result is a well-rounded community of believers working together. When serving one another in grace, something powerful happens; a compounding effect of God's work forms in our midst. A divine synergy emerges, greater than the sum of its parts. The banker, the stay-at-home parent, the builder, the pastor, the administrator, the student, and the exhorter all contributing their gifts to the health of the body.

Acts 4:33 provides a powerful example of this principle. Grace was not just a general force at work; each person carried a measure of it. "Great grace was upon them all". As each individual obeyed the Lord and operated in his or her calling, the result was exponential. Needs were met, and the presence of God was tangible. Heaven was touching earth, and what they experienced was an abundant supply until there was no more lack among them.

"Now the multitude of those who believed were of one heart and one soul; neither did anyone say that any of the things he possessed was his own, but they had all things in common. And with great power the apostles gave witness to the resurrection of the Lord Jesus. And great grace was upon them all. Nor was there anyone among them who lacked; for all who were possessors of lands or houses sold them, and brought the proceeds of the things that were sold, and laid them at the apostles' feet; and they distributed to each as anyone had need" (Acts 4:32-35).

When each person walks in his or her God-given grace, contributing from their unique identity and calling, the church becomes a thriving, united body. This is the power of divine grace at work within the people of God.

Reflection Questions

What is the difference between operating in God's grace and relying on natural talent or skill? Can you think of someone who walks in a grace-filled ability to serve God?

Ephesians 4:7-11 speaks of the fivefold ministry gifts. How has exposure to different ministry gifts (apostolic, prophetic, evangelistic, teaching, pastoral) impacted your spiritual growth?

Acts 4:32-35 describes a church where everyone contributed from their unique identity and calling. How does this challenge or inspire your view of the local church?

Grace, Leadership, and the Body of Christ

The grace of God empowers us in the areas where He has given us responsibility. Many wonder when they can expect God's grace to help them, especially during difficult seasons. Responsibility given by God comes with the grace to carry it out. It is not about ease or comfort but about His power working in and through us to accomplish His will.

Parents receive God's grace to lead and instruct their children. Those called to business receive grace to operate effectively in their industry and to do so with different values than the world. Ministry leaders are given grace for leadership, and those gifted with wisdom and counsel are empowered by His grace to fulfill their calling. Each person has access to God's grace in the areas where He has designed them to function.

"Having then gifts differing according to the grace that is given to us, let us use them: if prophecy, let us prophecy in proportion to our faith; or ministry, let us use it in our ministering; he who teaches, in teaching; he who exhorts, in exhortation; he who gives, with liberality; he who leads, with diligence; he who shows mercy, with cheerfulness" (Romans 12:6-8).

God has given each of us specific gifts by His grace so that we may fulfill our calling. In Ephesians 3:2, the Apostle Paul speaks in this way about the grace he received to minister to the Gentiles: "If indeed you have heard of the dispensation of the grace of God which was given to me for you".

Without understanding Paul's perspective on grace, this verse might make it sound like he was being arrogant. However, Paul understood that God had entrusted him with a unique grace to impart to the church. The people did not need his personal views or preferences; they needed the transformative power of God's grace working through him.

Paul urged the Corinthians to follow him as he followed Christ: "Imitate me, just as I also imitate Christ" (1 Corinthians 11:1).

They were to imitate Paul in the ways he imitated Christ, not in his personal habits or style. His goal was not to make people like himself, but to point them to Christ.

Paul understood the distinction between the grace God had given him and his own personality and opinions. In 1 Corinthians 7:12, when giving instructions on marriage, he even differentiates between his own thoughts and the Lord's commands.

In Galatians 4:19, Paul writes, "I labor until Christ is formed in you." His desire was not for people to follow his natural personality but to receive the grace of God upon his life so that they could be transformed into the image of Christ.

Many today seek friendship with leaders rather than the grace leaders carry. While relationships with leaders are valuable, what truly builds up is the impartation of the grace God has placed upon the leaders' lives for others.

This understanding should shape how we relate to leaders in our lives. God has placed something in them for us to receive. If we fail to recognize this, we may develop misplaced expectations, leading to disappointment when leaders do not meet our personal preferences and expectations. Some struggle with tension and mistrust any leader. When we fail to discern the grace of God in others' lives, we may become overly suspicious or critical. This mindset closes hearts and prevents us from receiving the portion God meant for us to receive through them. If we are only open to receive from leaders who share our culture, race, political views, or social status, we will miss much of what God has for us in the body of Christ.

Mentors and spiritual parents play a significant role in the lives of believers. The most valuable impartation they offer comes from the grace of God upon their lives. While they, like everyone, have personal opinions, habits, and preferences, these are not what should be sought after. It is the grace of God working through them that strengthens and builds others up.

Leaders carry a grace from God specifically for those they are called to lead. Every believer carries grace from the Lord that is intended to contribute to others. Just as the grace and spiritual gifts of leaders benefit those they serve, the grace of each believer is meant to flow to others. Receiving from the grace of God in another's life means focusing not on personal opinions or preferences, but on the way God is working through them.

This is the goal presented in Ephesians 4:11-16 for the life of the church. It was the reality in Acts 4:33, and it reflects what Jesus taught His disciples to pray in Matthew 6:10. God's kingdom would come and His will would be done on earth as it is in heaven.

"And He Himself gave some to be apostles, some prophets, some evangelists, and some pastors and teachers, for the equipping of the saints for the work of ministry, for the edifying of the body of Christ, till we all come to the unity of the faith and of the knowledge of the Son of God, to a perfect man, to the measure of the stature of the fullness of Christ; that we should no longer be children, tossed to and fro and carried about with every wind of doctrine, by the trickery of men, in the cunning craftiness of deceitful plotting, but, speaking the truth in love, may grow up in all things into Him who is the head—Christ—from whom the whole body, joined and knit together by what every joint supplies, according to the effective working by which every part does its share, causes growth of the body for the edifying of itself in love" (Ephesians 4:11-16).

Reflection Questions

How are you stewarding the grace God has given you to serve those around you? Ephesians 4:16 speaks of the church being built up by what "every joint supplies."

What happens when believers do not contribute their grace to the body of Christ?

Find a mentor or spiritual leader who carries a grace you want to grow in. Ask for wisdom, guidance, or prayer to help develop that area in your life.

Honoring God's Grace

"I, therefore, the prisoner of the Lord, beseech you to walk worthy of the calling with which you were called, with all lowliness and gentleness, with longsuffering, bearing with one another in love, endeavoring to keep the unity of the Spirit in the bond of peace" (Ephesians 4:1-3).

For the church to rise in unity and fully function in God's grace, a deep level of trust is required. The journey of faith calls for humility, gentleness, and patience among believers. Each person has a calling to fulfill, and as this passage states, the unity of the Spirit is already present in the church. However, it is the responsibility of believers to preserve this unity through peace.

This command is given because fulfilling God's purpose in each generation demands the collective effort of every believer working together in His grace. Trusting God as He works through imperfect vessels is essential. There are three key areas where trust must be exercised.

The first area is trusting in God's grace itself. God believes in His grace, and that it is sufficient to handle all human weaknesses and failures. Though people may falter, His grace never fails.

The second area of trust is that each one of us will need to learn to trust the way God's specific grace works in our own lives as we step out in faith. We will need to trust that God will meet us as we step out in faith. We learn to sharpen our senses and discernment in how God flows uniquely through us.

As Zechariah 4:6 states, "'Not by might nor by power, but by My Spirit,' Says the LORD of hosts."

Fulfilling God's will cannot be done through human strength alone but requires dependence on the Holy Spirit. It is our responsibility to both grow in trusting God's grace and making room for the Holy Spirit to flow through our lives. We must intentionally orient our lives so the grace of God can work through us. The modern lifestyle so often seems to resist providing the space for us to learn to make room for the flow of the grace of God. But when we value how God moves through us we will adapt our lives for the effectiveness of His grace.

God's grace is not for personal ambition or gain but for His purposes and His glory; we will need to trust His ways. In seeking His kingdom first; we find true fulfillment. Matthew 6:33 instructs, "But seek first the kingdom of God and His righteousness, and all these things shall be added to you."

The third area of trust involves recognizing and honoring the grace of God in others. Trusting in the grace given of God in others enables us to receive from the Lord through them and experience the strength and supply God provides through His people. Trusting in the grace of God that works through those God has placed in our lives allows us to receive inspiration and guidance toward maturity and effective ministry. As we commit to relationships within the body of Christ, we begin to understand how God moves through each member and can have faith for God to do so.

When a known prophetic minister came to our region, a colleague of mine reached out to him and simply said, "I know that God uses you to carry prophetic words. Would you pray and ask God if He will give you a word for me?" My friend was placing a righteous and healthy demand on the grace of God in this minister's life. This was not an unreasonable request at all. Now if my friend would have wanted this minister to provide something outside of the grace of God in his life, that would have been unreasonable. Place a healthy and righteous demand on the area of God's grace in people's lives and it will be a blessing to all. Place a demand outside of their area of grace and it will only cause unmet expectations and frustration for all involved.

Honor plays a key role in receiving from God through others. The principle of honor is that we are able to receive from that which we honor. When we acknowledge and honor the grace of God at work in others, it is able to impact and strengthen us in return.

It is crucial that we actively resist division. The enemy seeks to plant seeds of strife and division, especially toward leaders and other believers. He knows that if he can cause people to not receive from leadership he can stifle the equipping of the saints and the work of the ministry of the church. He knows that if he can turn believers against one another, the grace in their lives will lose its impact, weakening their witness and diminishing the church's testimony to the world.

The temptation to isolate must also be resisted, as Christian life is meant to be lived in fellowship. Separation from the body cuts us off from the grace that flows through others.

God's grace is sufficient for every challenge. Relying on His grace expands personal capacity, requiring faith and dependence on God. This journey demands an intentional lifestyle that prioritizes His grace and empowers believers to bear fruit in their gifts, callings, and purpose. Embracing this way of life means surrendering self-preservation as we allow His love, power, and grace to work through us to impact the world.

Reflection Questions

Why is it important to recognize and honor the grace of God in others? How does this change the way we receive from both leaders and fellow believers?

Have you seen division prevent the flow of God's grace in a church or ministry? What are practical ways to guard against this?

Zechariah 4:6 reminds us that God's work is done by His Spirit, not human effort. In what area of your life do you need to rely more on the Holy Spirit instead of your own strength?

ENDNOTES

1. https://christianhistoryinstitute.org/magazine/article/wesley-to-wilberforce

Great Grace

CHAPTER TEN

Remain in Grace

Eric Liddell, the Olympic gold medalist and missionary, is a powerful example of someone who focused on the grace of God by walking in his specific calling.

Liddell became famous for being a devoted follower of Christ who recognized that his athletic ability was a gift from God. He refused to compete in the 100-meter race at the 1924 Paris Olympics because it was scheduled on a Sunday, a day he had set apart for the Lord. Instead, he entered the 400-meter race—a distance he hadn't trained for extensively—and won gold. He later said the famous phrase:

"God made me fast. And when I run, I feel His pleasure."

But Liddell never let fame define him. He understood that his true calling was to be a missionary, and he left his athletic career behind to serve in China. Even in the face of hardship, imprisonment, and ultimately his death in a Japanese internment camp during World War II, he remained faithful to what God had called him to do.

He could have pursued fame and fortune in athletics, but he chose obedience over personal gain. His faithfulness serves as a beacon of encouragement to stay in God's grace and reject chasing worldly success that would take us out of that grace.

In 1925, following his Olympic success, Liddell returned to China to serve as a missionary with the London Missionary Society. He began his ministry in Tianjin (formerly Tientsin), where he taught science, English, and sports at the Anglo-Chinese College. This institution aimed to educate Chinese youth by integrating Western scientific knowledge with Christian principles. Liddell's role extended beyond academics; he also supervised the Sunday school at Union Church, where his father had been a pastor.

In 1941, as tensions escalated due to Japanese aggression, Liddell chose to remain in China while his family relocated to Canada for safety. He moved to Xiaozhang, a rural mission station in Hebei province, to assist his brother Rob, a medical doctor. There, Liddell engaged in evangelistic work, often traveling by foot or bicycle to reach remote villages, embodying his commitment to serving impoverished communities.

During World War II, Liddell was interned by Japanese forces at the Weihsien Internment Camp in 1943. Despite the harsh conditions, he became a leader and organizer within the camp, teaching science and Bible classes, arranging sports activities, and providing support to fellow internees. His selflessness and unwavering faith left a lasting impression on those around him.

Eric Liddell's missionary endeavors exemplify a profound dedication to his faith and the people of China, demonstrating a life committed to service beyond personal accolades. [1]

Endurance through Grace

"Therefore, since we are receiving a kingdom which cannot be shaken, let us have grace, by which we may serve God acceptably with reverence and godly fear" (Hebrews 12:28).

God's grace not only empowers believers to endure difficulties but also positions us to thrive, firmly established in God. Peter describes this process in 1 Peter 5:10: "But may the God of all grace, who called us to His eternal glory by Christ Jesus, after you have suffered a while, perfect, establish, strengthen, and settle you."

This verse paints a powerful picture of what God can do when believers remain steadfast through challenges. Life's challenges will arise, but remaining in God's grace prevents stagnation and builds the spiritual muscle of endurance. We often need to be reminded and encouraged to remain in faith, especially during the difficult days in life's journey. How encouraging to read that the same grace that strengthens us to come through suffering will also perfect, establish, strengthen, and settle us!

Acts 13:43 recounts Paul and Barnabas speaking to the devout Jews and proselytes in Antioch, stating that they "persuaded them to continue in the grace of God." There are moments in life when encouragement is needed to continue in His grace.

One particularly discouraging season in my life involved me sitting on the side of the road beside my broken-down car. After years of ministry among refugees in Cape Town, a series of betrayals and financial hardships had taken their toll. Some leaders I once looked up to let us down, lies had been spread, and some supporters withdrew their financial partnership. Barely surviving month to month, my frustration reached a breaking point. Attempts to fix the car had only made things worse, and in that moment of exhaustion, tears of anger and weariness flowed. The question arose—why was this season so difficult? What were we doing wrong?

Looking back, the decision to persevere through that season was life-changing. Even in the darkest hours, God's grace was still flowing. Eventually, the season shifted, leading to a time of immense blessing in ministry.

Another challenging period in our lives arose while working to grow a church in the inner city context. Ideas that had appeared promising to bring more people to Christ were not working. Despite our best efforts, leadership strategies I had learned in my home country did not translate well into our current cultural context. Yet even in my moments of feeling frustrated, God's grace was moving. He was faithful to provide content for me to preach and in times of prayer people were still getting healed, set free and delivered.

In hindsight, those difficult seasons were instrumental in shaping my character, fostering humility, and refining my purpose. They were not obstacles but opportunities for deeper reliance on God's wisdom and personal exploration. I didn't know it then, but God was developing spiritual muscles that I didn't even know needed developing. These disappointing moments were actually setting the stage for some amazing discoveries in Christ. Over time, through His grace, new strategies emerged that brought fruitfulness and growth.

Hard times seek to dislodge believers from remaining in God's grace. Endurance and perseverance are necessary to remain in His calling, even when circumstances are difficult or we are plagued with doubts and fears. Holding onto His grace ensures that every challenge ultimately serves as a stepping stone to a greater purpose.

"For you have need of endurance, so that after you have done the will of God, you may receive the promise" (Hebrews 10:36).

Reflection Questions

How have challenges in your life shaped your character and deepened your reliance on God?

What unexpected growth or maturity did you learn in those difficult seasons?

Grace, Growth and Preparation

Consider Joseph in the book of Genesis (chapters 37-50), He had a divine gift from God to interpret dreams. However, his leadership and management abilities were cultivated under his father, Jacob. Jacob himself had gone from having nothing to stewarding and managing great wealth, and Joseph absorbed that wisdom.

Wherever Joseph found himself, whether in prison or later as a ruler over Egypt, his leadership and management skills were evident. The grace of God in his life was to lead and govern, and his supernatural gift of dream interpretation worked in harmony with the skills he developed. His time in his father's house was a season of preparation and sharpening his abilities so that when the moment of destiny arrived, he was ready to step into it.

A grace to lead in certain areas still requires development. Like the maturing of any gift from God, it is not enough to simply recognize gifting; there must be an active cultivation of the gift. This involves turning raw potential into refined skill. In charismatic ministries, there can be a tendency to overlook the natural process of growth and development. When God gives someone a vision or a calling, it can be easy to assume that they are ready to walk in it fully. However, no one arrives fully prepared, no matter how gifted they are. God's grace empowers learning, growth, and equipping for the assignments He has given.

For example, I have a friend that is a medical doctor. It is part of God's grace for her life. But a medical doctor does not simply walk into a hospital and start practicing medicine. Years of study, training, and practice are required. God's grace does not eliminate the need for the process; it empowers the individual to go through it successfully.

The same principle applies to all areas of calling. A preacher may take a public speaking course to sharpen communication skills and dive deeper into theology to strengthen biblical understanding. A worship leader with a naturally strong voice may take vocal lessons to refine technique, supporting the ability to lead worship for extended periods without strain.

A leader may read books, attend conferences, and seek mentorship to grow in the ability to lead people well. A business owner may network with other business owners to expand industry knowledge. A stay-at-home parent may connect with other parents, read books, or learn from those who have already raised their children well.

Regardless of the specific grace placed on a life, there is always room to grow. Stewarding God's calling requires embracing the journey of learning and development, trusting that His grace is not just for the destination but also for the process.

Reflection Questions

In what areas of your calling do you sense the need for growth, and how can you actively embrace the learning process?

How can you shift your perspective to see God's grace not just as a means to an end but as a sustaining force throughout your journey?

What practical steps can you take to strengthen yourself in the areas where God has called you to serve?

Responding to Disappointment with Grace

One of the hardest challenges in life is dealing with disappointment, especially when it comes from people who are trusted. In a fallen world, even the best individuals remain imperfect vessels. A boss may fail to meet expectations, a close friend may betray trust, a church leader may falter, or a parent may not provide the guidance hoped for. At times people are exposed for doing terrible things. The writer of Hebrews calls it "falling short of the grace of God." The question is, how should one respond when disappointment arises?

The writer of Hebrews provides clear direction:

"Pursue peace with all people, and holiness, without which no one will see the Lord: looking carefully lest anyone fall short of the grace of God; lest any root of bitterness springing up cause trouble, and by this many become defiled" (Hebrews 12:14-15).

When someone falls short of God's grace, it can open the door to bitterness and trouble. We must be vigilant, ensuring that another's shortcoming does not lead us to stray from God's grace as well.

Even in seasons of difficulty, scripture calls believers to pursue peace and holiness. If we allow offenses to take root, the stirring up of division, or respond in unrighteousness, we risk missing the deeper work God desires to accomplish through the trial.

The passage warns that bitterness can cause us to fall short of God's grace. Bitterness is not an isolated issue. It spreads, defiling others along the way. This is why guarding the heart and refusing to let offense or disappointment steal God's grace is crucial.

Reacting to frustration with anger or compromising integrity in response to hurt can destroy the very thing God's grace is building. Paul offers an example of how to stay grounded.

"For our boasting is this: the testimony of our conscience that we conducted ourselves in the world in simplicity and godly sincerity, not with fleshly wisdom but by the grace of God, and more abundantly toward you" (2 Corinthians 1:12).

Paul and his companions did not respond to hardship with worldly wisdom or fleshly reactions. Instead, they chose to walk in simplicity and godly sincerity, relying on God's grace to guide their actions. This same approach must be taken today. We are called to choose grace over resentment and righteousness over retaliation.

Peter reminds believers that trials refine, just as fire purifies gold. During these refining seasons, he gives a key instruction:

"Therefore gird up the loins of your mind, be sober, and rest your hope fully upon the grace that is to be brought to you at the revelation of Jesus Christ" (1 Peter 1:13).

In modern terms, "gird up the loins of your mind" could be understood as "pull yourself together" or "take control of your thoughts." Trials can easily lead to negative thinking, doubt, and frustration. However, Peter challenges believers to anchor hope fully in God's grace rather than in emotions or circumstances.

Disappointment is inevitable, but the response to it is a choice. Instead of allowing bitterness to take root, peace and holiness must be pursued. Instead of reacting in the flesh, reliance on God's grace is essential. Instead of letting thoughts spiral into negativity, they must be aligned with His truth.

By doing so, believers remain positioned to walk in God's purpose—refined, strengthened, and filled with His grace.

Reflection Questions

Have you ever allowed bitterness to take root in your heart? How did it affect your relationship with God and others?

1 Peter 1:13 tells us to fully rest our hope on the grace of Jesus Christ. How does shifting your hope from people to God's grace change your perspective on disappointment?

Strength in God's Grace

Paul instructs the young leader Timothy to be strong in the grace found in Christ. "You therefore, my son, be strong in the grace that is in Christ Jesus" (2 Timothy 2:1).

Paul knew that Timothy would need God's grace for the work ahead. He then instructs Timothy to take what he has been taught and pass it on to others who will, in turn, teach others.

"What you have heard from me in the presence of many witnesses, commit to faithful men who will be able to teach others also" (2 Timothy 2: 2).

The grace of God moving through Timothy's life would impact many. While Timothy was undoubtedly a capable and intelligent leader, Paul saw the importance of reminding him to be strong in God's grace. The Greek word used here means to be empowered and can be specifically translated as continually increasing in strength through God's grace.

Paul was emphasizing the need for Timothy to be intentional about drawing strength from God's grace. He knew challenges would come, testing Timothy beyond his own abilities.

In the same passage, Paul urges Timothy to endure hardship like a good soldier, an athlete, and a hardworking farmer. A soldier follows the commands of a superior, an athlete trains with focus and competes by the rules, and a farmer works diligently through all seasons, tending the crops until the harvest. Each of these roles comes with struggles: the soldier faces battles, the athlete endures fatigue, exercise and competition, and the farmer overcomes adverse conditions in order to reap a harvest. None of them can afford to be distracted by the concerns of the world. Doing so would divert their attention and dilute their effectiveness. By continually growing in God's grace, Timothy would be equipped to persevere. Paul wanted Timothy to be an example of a leader who relies on God's grace and mentors others to do the same.

Character is essential for sustaining what God builds. If our character does not align with the work God is doing, it will eventually be exposed, potentially leading to the downfall of what was built. A lack of integrity can ultimately destroy what God's grace had empowered to be established.

This principle extends beyond leadership to every believer. Every individual has areas for growth, whether it be blind spots or struggles that need to be addressed. It is vitally important to address the hindrances that affect one's testimony. When personal struggles overshadow God's grace, others may find it difficult to receive from what He is doing through that person. A harsh demeanor, lack of integrity, or ongoing struggles with destructive behaviors can obscure a testimony, making it harder for others to recognize and embrace God's grace through that individual.

God's grace works through imperfect vessels, but unchecked character flaws can harm a testimony and become a barrier to others receiving that grace. To ensure His grace flows through us unhindered, we must consistently align our lives with the specific ways He chooses to work in and through us. When we intentionally orient our schedules, resources, and daily choices around His grace, we create space for God to work through us, allowing others to freely receive. We are called to live in a way that keeps us anchored in His grace.

Reflection Questions

What personal struggles or blind spots might be hindering your testimony, and how can you invite God's grace to bring transformation in those areas of your life?

How can you intentionally align your daily choices, schedule, and resources with God's grace to ensure His work flows freely through your life?

Living in the Overflow of God's Grace

The great grace of God described in Acts 4:33 is available to the entire church today. Each person has a vital role to play. As believers express lives of faith in what God can do and passionately become vessels of His life and power, and strategically live for His grace to have maximum effect, God's kingdom will manifest powerfully in our communities.

God's work in the lives of His people is not finished. There is more! As each believer is empowered by the Holy Spirit to carry out God's will, the grace of God flowing through them will transform communities. Churches will become places of life and vitality, not only because of powerful leaders, but as each individual contributes their unique expression of grace. God's work will be known, and His name will be glorified.

The supply of God's grace is meant to be lived in and experienced. His abundant heart pours out over His people daily. His desire is for each person to experience the full measure of His grace and to share it with others. Every believer has a specific call and purpose, and His grace empowers each of us.

Eternity with God will be beyond comparison, but bringing His kingdom to earth and expressing His divine will in this life is the mission of this generation. May the powerful flow of the living water of God's Spirit bubble forth, making His love known to the world. As faith reaches into the vast measure of His grace, a cumulative, compounding effect will take place through the lives of His saints, impacting the world in ways yet unseen.

Churches will overflow with expressions of God's kingdom, reflecting the examples seen in the book of Acts. Homes, cities, and nations will be blessed as God's heart is experienced in meaningful ways. As faith is directed toward receiving God's grace, growing in understanding, being trained by it, and remaining steadfast in it, the world will be forever changed for the glory of God.

Church communities will come alive with the dynamic movement of God's grace flowing through each individual, creating an environment of abundance that resources all He desires to accomplish in this generation.

"For your fellowship in the gospel from the first day until now, being confident of this very thing, that He who has begun a good work in you will complete it until the day of Jesus Christ; just as it is right for me to think this of you all, because I have you in my heart, inasmuch as both in my chains and in the defense and confirmation of the gospel, you all are partakers with me of grace" (Philippians 1:5-7).

Reflection Questions

Philippians 1:5-7 says believers are partakers of grace together. How does sharing in God's grace with others deepen relationships and strengthen the body of Christ? How has God uniquely gifted and graced you to contribute to the church?

Philippians 1:6 reminds us that He who began a good work in you will complete it. How does this truth encourage you in seasons where you feel unfinished or unqualified?

Ask the Holy Spirit to highlight one area in your life where He wants you to trust Him for more of His grace. Write it down and take one step of faith toward walking in that grace this week.

ENDNOTES

1. https://www.chinasource.org/resource-library/chinese-church-voices/the-olympic-champion-with-a-heart-for-china/
https://www.churchofscotland.org.uk/news-and-events/news/articles/olympians-missionary-legacy-in-china-explored
https://www.bdcconline.net/en/stories/liddell-eric-henry/
https://en.wikipedia.org/wiki/Eric_Liddell

Chapter 1 Outline
Great Grace

1. **Experiencing God's Grace**
   - **Divine Encounters Transform Lives**
     - Personal experiences shift grace from a concept to a revelation.
     - God's grace empowers beyond personal ability.
     - 2 Corinthians 12:9 "My grace is sufficient for you, for My strength is made perfect in weakness."
   - **A Foundational Revelation of Grace**
     - Personal testimony of serving as a worship director
     - Encounter with God's tangible peace and supernatural supply
     - Recognizing divine impartations of grace
   - **Dependence on God's Supply**
     - Ministry flows powerfully when relying on God rather than personal effort.
     - Romans 13:14 "Put on the Lord Jesus Christ, and make no provision for the flesh."
     - Surrender and alignment allow for an unrestricted flow of grace.

2. **Great Grace Was upon Them All**
   - **Grace and Power Work Together**
     - Acts 4:33 "And with great power the apostles gave witness... And great grace was upon them all."
     - Grace and power enable believers to witness and minister effectively.
   - **The Reality of God's Grace Today**
     - The early church's experience is not a one-time event.

- Matthew 6:10 "Your kingdom come, Your will be done on earth as it is in heaven."
- The apostles understood the fullness of what was available in Christ.

- **Grace in the Midst of Persecution**
  - The disciples, despite opposition, stood firm in faith.
  - Prayer led to a fresh infilling of the Holy Spirit.
  - Acts 4:34-35 "Nor was there anyone among them who lacked… they distributed to each as anyone had need."
  - Unity and selflessness marked the early church's great grace.

3. **The Power of Grace Synergy**
   - **God's Grace Produces Abundance**
     - 2 Corinthians 9:8 "God is able to make all grace abound… always having all sufficiency in all things."
     - Grace ensures provision for every good work—beyond finances.
   - **Paul's Experience of Abounding**
     - Philippians 4:12 "I know how to be abased, and I know how to abound."
     - The early church experienced ongoing generosity.
   - **Grace Activates Every Believer**
     - The body of Christ flourishes when all members function together.
     - Ministry is not reserved for a select few—it's for all who receive grace.
     - Ephesians 4:16 "From whom the whole body, joined and knit together… causes growth of the body for the edifying of itself in love."

- **Grace Creates Divine Synergy**
  - When each believer operates in their gifts, unity forms.
  - The church moves in supernatural power, reflecting heaven on earth.
  - Acts 4:32 "Now the multitude of those who believed were of one heart and one soul."

Conclusion: Living in Great Grace

- Grace is more than a concept—it is a living reality.
- Every believer is called to walk in and release the grace of God.
- As we align ourselves with His presence, grace flows in power and provision.

Call to Action

Seek, receive, and release God's great grace in your life and community.

Final Scripture

Hebrews 4:16 "Let us therefore come boldly to the throne of grace, that we may obtain mercy and find grace to help in time of need."

Chapter 2 Outline
God's Gift

1. ## Understanding God's Grace as a Gift
   - **Grace as a Transformative Experience**
     - Hebrews 12:1 "Faith as the substance of things hoped for."
     - 1 Peter 3:15 "Always be prepared to give an answer for the hope we have."

2. ## Christianity 101: The Foundation of Grace
   - **Grace and Salvation**
     - Ephesians 2:8-9 "Salvation is a gift of grace, not by works."
     - Grace is God's work; it's not earned but freely given.
     - Distinction between grace and mercy:
       - MERCY: Not getting what we deserve.
       - GRACE: Receiving what we do not deserve.
   - **Illustration: The Courtroom Analogy**
     - MERCY: The Judge forgives the fine.
     - GRACE: The judge provides a lifetime of transportation and a watch.

3. ## The Radical Nature of God's Grace
   - **The Thief on the Cross (Luke 23:41-43)**
     - No opportunity for good works, yet received grace through faith
     - Grace is scandalous to the religious mindset.
     - Philippians 3:9 – Righteousness comes through faith, not our efforts.

Chapter 2 Outline: God's Gift

4. **God's Grace Is Not Based on Feelings**
   - **Struggles with Doubt and Condemnation**
     o John Newton's transformation and the hymn "Amazing Grace"
     o 1 John 3:20 (TPT) – God is greater than our self-condemnation.
   - **Enemy's Tactics: Condemnation and Shame**
     o He lies that grace is too good to be true.
     o Truth: Righteousness is a gift received at salvation.
     o Quote: "Believers need to stop trying to get something they already have!"
   - **The Role of God's Word Over Feelings**
     o Feelings reflect what we believe, not necessarily the truth.
     o The church must stand on God's Word, not emotions.

5. **New Identity in Christ**
   - **Becoming a New Creation**
     o Salvation transforms us from sinners to sons and daughters.
     o 2 Corinthians 5:17 – Old things have passed away, all things become new.
     o Ephesians 2:10 – Created for good works prepared by God
   - **Living as a Child of God**
     o Our identity does not change based on performance.
     o We remain saved by grace on our best and worst days.
   - **Purpose beyond Salvation**
     o The Gospel is more than just forgiveness—it's about a transformed life.
     o Demonstrating God's kingdom on earth through our lives

Chapter 3 Outline
The Kingdom Gospel

1. **The Gospel of the Kingdom**
   - **Baptism as Full Immersion in God**
     - Matthew 28:19 – Command to baptize in the name of the Father, Son, and Holy Spirit.
     - Mark 16:16 – Baptism as an act of faith leading to salvation
     - Illustration: Transformation of a cucumber into a pickle, signifying complete immersion in God's presence
     - True discipleship goes beyond intellectual agreement to full transformation.
   - **Jesus Preached the Gospel Before the Cross**
     - Mark 1:14-15 – Jesus preached the gospel of the kingdom.
     - Matthew 4:23 – Jesus demonstrated the kingdom through healing and miracles.
     - The gospel is not just personal spirituality but affects all of life.

2. **The Kingdom Rejected in Eden**
   - **The Fall of Humanity**
     - Adam and Eve rejected God's rule by choosing self-rule.
     - Satan's deception: God's ways are restrictive and untrustworthy.
     - This deception persists today in philosophies that reject God's design for life.
   - **The Consequences of Rejecting God's Reign**
     - Humanity experienced separation from God's kingdom.

Chapter 3 Outline: The Kingdom Gospel

- o God initiated the Old and New Covenants as a way to draw people back.
- o Religious traditions distorted God's law, creating barriers to His kingdom (Matthew 23:13).

3. **Jesus' Call to the Kingdom**
   - **The Good News of the Kingdom**
     - o Jesus' message called people to return to God's reign.
     - o His sacrifice on the cross reversed the effects of the fall.
     - o Many still reject God's rulership, leading to brokenness.
     - o Our mission: Preach and demonstrate the gospel, just as Jesus did.

4. **Living the Full Gospel of the Kingdom**
   - **Jesus Modeled the Kingdom Life**
     - o His life was a demonstration of complete surrender to God's will.
     - o He countered false narratives about God's character.
     - o His teachings in Matthew 5-7 outline kingdom living.

5. **The Full Picture of Biblical Salvation**
   - **Justification**
     - o Instant salvation upon turning to Jesus (Ephesians 2:8-9)
     - o Made righteous before God
   - **Sanctification**
     - o Ongoing transformation through obedience (Philippians 2:12, Romans 12:2)
     - o The process of becoming like Christ (2 Corinthians 3:18)
     - o Living in surrender under God's kingdom

- **Glorification**
  - Future transformation at Christ's return (1 Corinthians 15:42-43, Philippians 3:21)

6. **The Three Parts of Salvation**

    - **1 John 3:2-3 and 1 Thessalonians 5:23 highlight justification, sanctification, and glorification.**

    - **Grace is not just for initial salvation but a continuous flow of empowerment.**

    - **Living in grace ensures victory, renewal, and fulfillment of God's purpose.**

Chapter 4 Outline
Empowering Grace

1. **Grace in Every Season**
   - **God's Grace Sustains through Hardship**
     - Temptations to adopt a victim mindset, but God's grace provides strength.
     - Encouragement from others as an extension of God's grace.
   - **God's Grace in Practical Matters**
     - Example of receiving supernatural wisdom for problem-solving
     - Grace extends beyond spiritual matters into everyday challenges.
   - **The Throne of Grace**
     - Hebrews 4:16 – Approach the throne of grace with confidence.
     - God's grace is always available, offering divine advantage in every situation.

2. **The Live Wire of God's Grace**
   - **Grace as a Constant Power Source**
     - Grace as an active, continuous flow, like a live electrical wire
     - Connection to Jesus is the life-giving flow of grace.
   - **Grace Teaches and Transforms**
     - Titus 2:11-13 – Grace teaches believers to deny ungodliness and live righteously.
     - Hebrews 10:29 – The Holy Spirit is the Spirit of grace.
   - **Grace vs. Human Effort**
     - Attempting to live righteously without grace leads to striving and legalism.

- Illustration: Two trees in the Garden—Tree of Life (relationship with God) vs. Tree of Knowledge of Good and Evil (self-reliance).
- True transformation comes from a relational connection with God.

3. **The River and the Trees**
    - **Grace as a River**
        - Ezekiel 47 – The river of God's presence brings life and healing.
        - Trees by the river bear fruit continually, symbolizing a constant effect of grace.
    - **Jesus, the Source of Living Water**
        - John 7:37-39 – The Holy Spirit as rivers of living water.
        - Psalm 46:4 – God's river makes glad the city of God.
        - Psalm 1:1-3 – The righteous flourish like trees planted by rivers of water.
    - **Living in the Flow of Grace**
        - The river represents God's abundant provision for believers.
        - Staying rooted in grace ensures constant spiritual nourishment and fruitfulness.

4. **Abiding in the Vine: Living in the Life Flow of Grace**
    - **Jesus as the Vine**
        - John 15:5 – Abiding in Christ leads to fruitfulness.
        - The command is not to produce fruit but to stay connected to the Vine.
    - **Faith as the Connection to Grace**
        - Hebrews 11:6 – Faith pleases God and connects us to His grace.

Chapter 4 Outline: Empowering Grace

- o   Living inside faith ensures the lifeflow of grace.
- **Avoiding Spiritual Disconnect**
    - o   Religious duty vs. relational dependence.
    - o   Works done outside of faith lack life and do not please God.
    - o   Abiding in Jesus ensures a continual supply of grace, leading to true transformation and fruitfulness.

Chapter 5 Outline
Accessing Grace

1. **God's Grace Is His Abundant Supply**
   - **Living under God's Provision**
     - 2 Corinthians 9:8 – God's grace is all-sufficient and overflowing.
     - Ezekiel's river as a metaphor for God's abundant grace
   - **Grace in Challenges**
     - Romans 8:37 – "More than conquerors" through God's love
     - Greek term *hupernikao* meaning "hyper-victory"
     - Example: Joseph's vine growing over obstacles (Genesis 49:22)
     - Paul's endurance through hardships as a testament to grace

2. **Sufficient Grace**
   - **God's Power in Weakness**
     - 2 Corinthians 12:9-10 "My grace is sufficient for you."
     - Weakness magnifies the power of Christ.
     - Illustration: Samson's strength revealing God's power
     - Gideon's small army ensuring God receives the glory
   - **God Uses Ordinary People**
     - The misconception that effective ministers have special abilities
     - True success comes from total reliance on God.
     - Paul's "thorn in the flesh" did not hinder his mission; instead, grace empowered him.

Chapter 5 Outline: Accessing Grace

3. **Here for All**
   - **Grace Available to Everyone**
     - John 1:16 – "Of His fullness we have all received, and grace for grace."
     - "Universal grace" – available to all who respond.
     - 2 Corinthians 6:1 – "Do not receive the grace of God in vain."
   - **Engaging with God's Grace**
     - The Corinthians received grace but failed to live in its power.
     - Grace must be actively received and expressed.
     - Believers must apply faith to explore and grow in grace.

Chapter 6 Outline
Faith and Grace

1. **Grace in Everyday Life**
   - **Experiencing God's Grace in Practical Matters**
     - Recognizing God's provision beyond spiritual encounters.
     - Trusting God's guiding hand in daily challenges.

2. **Accessing God's Grace**
   - **Faith as the Key to Grace**
     - Ephesians 2:6-8 – Grace is received through faith.
     - Romans 5:2 – "Access by faith into this grace"
     - Spiritual gifts as manifestations of grace (Romans 12:6)
   - **Faith Determines the Flow of Grace**
     - Misunderstanding of spiritual gifts as fixed abilities vs. manifestations
     - Faith must grow to access more of God's grace.

3. **Strengthening Faith by Remembering God's Faithfulness**
   - **Faith Must Be Applied According to God's Word**
     - Faith aligns thoughts and emotions with God's grace.
     - King David's practice of remembering God's past faithfulness (Psalm 77)
   - **Personal Example: Facing Spiritual Warfare**
     - Writing down past testimonies to recall God's faithfulness
     - Faith connects us to the ongoing work of God's grace.

Chapter 6 Outline: Faith and Grace

4. **Growing in Faith for Grace**
   - **Faith as a Connection to God's Supply**
     - Luke 17:5 – "Lord, increase our faith."
     - Faith must grow to match the intensity of life's challenges.
   - **Personal Testimony: A Season of Testing**
     - Trusting in God's provision despite overwhelming circumstances.
     - Romans 8:28 – God working all things for good

5. **Grace in Hardship**
   - **God's Grace Holds Us Together**
     - Hebrews 4:16 – "Grace to help in time of need."
     - The Greek term "help" refers to frapping a ship—binding it together in storms.
     - 2 Corinthians 4:7 – "Treasure in earthen vessels."

4. **Growing in Faith Through Prayer**
   - **Praying in the Holy Spirit Strengthens Faith**
     - Jude 1:20 – "Building yourselves up on your most holy faith, praying in the Holy Spirit"
     - 1 Corinthians 14:14 – Praying in tongues edifies the believer.
   - **The Power of Spirit-Led Prayer**
     - Distinguishing between personal prayer language and public messages in tongues
     - Aligning faith with God's will rather than relying on human reasoning

Chapter 7 Outline
Growing in Grace

1. Growing in the Holy Spirit
   - **Experiencing the Move of the Holy Spirit**
     - o Importance of surrounding oneself with Spirit-filled believers
     - o Seeking deeper experiences of the Holy Spirit
   - **Luke 11:9-13 – Asking for More of the Holy Spirit**
2. Increase Our Faith
   - **Faith Grows through Hearing God's Word**
     - o Romans 10:17 – "Faith comes by hearing."
     - o Deuteronomy 6:4-5 – Truly hearing means obeying.
     - o Filtering truth through Scripture in a world of competing narratives.
3. The Power of Active Faith
   - **Faith as an Ongoing Process**
     - o Romans 10:17 – "Hearing" is in present tense, indicating continual listening.
     - o John 10:27 – "My sheep listen to My voice."
     - o Avoiding reliance on formulas; seeking God's direction in each situation
4. Removing Barriers to God's Grace
   - **Avoiding "Dimmer Switches" on God's Power**
     - o Restrictions of our faith act like dimmers on God's grace.
     - o Matthew 5:15-16 "Let your light shine before men."

Chapter 7 Outline: Growing in Grace

5. **Grace, Truth, and Repentance**
    - **John 1:17 – "Grace and Truth Came through Jesus"**
        - Avoiding the extremes of "grace" without truth or "truth" without grace
    - **Genuine repentance leads to transformation.**

6. **Humility and Faith: Keys to Greater Grace**
    - **James 4:6 – "God Gives Grace to the Humble"**
        - Humility increases grace in our lives.
        - Balance of humility and bold faith in mature believers

7. **Growing in Grace**
    - **2 Peter 3:18 – Growing in Grace and Knowledge**
        - God's grace is abundant, but we must grow in receiving it.
        - Faith expands our ability to experience more of His grace.
        - Illustration: Growing into spiritual "clothes" of grace

8. **Carriers of God's Grace**
    - **God's Presence Rests on People, Not Systems**
        - 2 Samuel 6 – Lessons from transporting the Ark of the Covenant
        - God's grace flows through obedient, surrendered lives.

Chapter 8 Outline
Specialized Grace

1. **Impartation and Activation**
   - **Receiving from Spiritual Mentors**
     - Learning from those with deep experiences with God (Proverbs 13:20)
     - Surrounding ourselves with those who strengthen our faith (Hebrews 10:24-25)
   - **Integration of Theology and Practical Experience**
     - True equipping goes beyond intellectual understanding to action. (James 1:22)
     - Some principles are "caught" more than taught. (2 Timothy 2:2)
   - **Running with the Hungry**
     - Connecting with those passionate for God (Psalm 63:1-2)
     - Faith is strengthened by witnessing God's work in others. (Romans 1:11-12)

2. **The Power behind Our Calling**
   - **Grace as Power and Authority**
     - Grace is not only salvation but also empowerment. (1 Corinthians 15:10)
     - Jesus operated in unity with the Father. (John 5:19)
   - **Grace for Unique Callings**
     - Paul and Barnabas had a grace for the Gentiles. (Galatians 2:9)
     - Grace is both universal and personally tailored. (Ephesians 4:7)
     - The grace on our lives is observable to others. (Acts 11:23)

Chapter 8 Outline: Specialized Grace

3. **Grace, Identity, and Calling**
   - **Spiritual Growth and Discernment**
     - Our senses are sharpened through use. (Hebrews 5:14)
     - We are on a journey of discovering gifts and callings. (Ephesians 2:10)
   - **Universal Principles and Personal Application**
     - Biblical principles apply universally, but our walk with God is unique. (1 Peter 4:10)
     - Using God-given talents for His glory brings fulfillment. (Colossians 3:23-24)

4. **Finding Your Sweet Spot in God's Grace**
   - **Aligning Talents, Calling, and Grace**
     - God's grace empowers us to fulfill our purpose. (Acts 17:27)
     - Convergence: Natural talents + spiritual gifts + divine opportunities
   - **Success Redefined**
     - True success is being in God's presence. (Matthew 6:33)
     - Paul's sweet spot was the Gentiles, though counterintuitive. (Acts 22:3, Galatians 1:15-16)
     - God calls us beyond our comfort zones. (2 Corinthians 12:9-10, Acts 4:13)

5. **Grace and Sabbath**
   - **The Necessity of Rest**
     - The anointing does not replace the need for physical and emotional renewal. (Exodus 20:8-10)
     - Jesus practiced withdrawing for rest and prayer. (Luke 5:16)

- **Keeping the Sabbath Holy**
  - Sabbath is not just personal rest but communion with God. (Mark 2:27)
  - Trusting God in rest is an act of faith. (Matthew 11:28-30)
- **Stewarding Ourselves Well**
  - Balancing work, ministry, and personal renewal (1 Corinthians 15:10)
  - The rhythm of rest enables sustained effectiveness in God's grace. (Isaiah 40:31)

Chapter 9 Outline
Trusting God's Grace

1. **Grace through One Another**
   - **God Raises Up Individuals with His Grace**
     - John Wesley's encouragement to William Wilberforce.
     - 1 Corinthians 3:10 - God's grace enables us to build upon the foundation of Christ.
   - **Grace Does Not Mean Ease**
     - Hardships do not indicate the absence of grace.
     - Titus 2:11-12 - Grace brings salvation and trains us for godly living.
   - **Recognizing Grace in Others**
     - Grace enables believers to serve beyond natural abilities.
     - Ephesians 4:7-11 - Fivefold ministry gifts equip and build up the body.
     - Acts 4:32-35 - The early church flourished as grace worked in each member.

2. **Grace, Leadership, and the Body of Christ**
   - **God's Grace Empowers Responsibility**
     - Believers receive grace to fulfill their callings.
     - Romans 12:6-8 - Different gifts are given according to God's grace.
   - **Paul's Understanding of Grace**
     - Ephesians 3:2 - Paul was entrusted with grace to minister to the Gentiles.
     - 1 Corinthians 11:1 - Paul urged believers to imitate his Christ-centered life.
   - **Receiving Grace from Leaders**
     - Leaders are vessels of God's grace, not just friends or role models.

- Galatians 4:19 - Paul labored for Christ to be formed in believers.
- Discerning grace in others prevents division and enhances spiritual growth.

3. **Honoring God's Grace**
    - **Walking Worthy of Our Calling**
        - Ephesians 4:1-3 - Maintain unity in the Spirit through humility and patience.
    - **Trusting in God's Grace**
        - Zechariah 4:6 - God's work is done by His Spirit, not by human effort.
        - Matthew 6:33 - Seek first the kingdom, and all things will be provided.
    - **Recognizing Grace in Others**
        - Placing a healthy demand on the grace in others' lives.
        - Honoring leaders and fellow believers allows God's grace to flow freely.
    - **Guarding against Division**
        - The enemy seeks to divide believers to hinder the work of grace.
        - Isolation prevents believers from receiving and contributing grace.
        - Acts 4:33 - "Great grace was upon them all," leading to unity and provision.

Chapter 10 Outline
Remain in Grace

1. **Living in God's Grace: The Example of Eric Liddell**
   - **Eric Liddell's Commitment to Grace and Calling**
     o Olympic gold medalist and missionary
     o Prioritized obedience to God over worldly success
   - **His Missionary Work in China**
     o Taught and evangelized in China despite hardships
     o Remained in an internment camp during WWII, serving others

2. **Endurance through Grace**
   - **Hebrews 12:28 - Receiving an Unshakable Kingdom**
     o God's grace enables believers to endure and serve faithfully.
     o 1 Peter 5:10 - God strengthens and establishes after suffering.
   - **Encouragement to Continue in Grace**
     o Acts 13:43 - Paul and Barnabas urged believers to remain in grace.
     o Life's challenges are not signs of abandonment but opportunities for growth.
   - **Personal Testimonies of Enduring through Challenges**
     o Difficult seasons teach reliance on God's wisdom.
     o Hardships develop spiritual endurance and character.

3. **Grace, Growth, and Preparation**
   - **Joseph's Example: Preparation for His Calling**
     o Interpreting dreams was a divine gift, but leadership skills were developed.

- Time in his father's house prepared him for governance.
- **The Process of Growth in God's Grace**
  - Grace empowers learning and development
  - Stewarding God's calling requires growth and refinement.
- **Applying this Principle in Different Callings**
  - Spiritual gifts should be developed alongside natural skills.

4. **Responding to Disappointment with Grace**
   - **Hebrews 12:14-15 - Avoiding Bitterness**
     - Offenses can cause people to fall short of God's grace.
   - **Paul's Example: Conducting Life in Simplicity and Grace**
     - 2 Corinthians 1:12 - Paul relied on grace rather than fleshly wisdom.
   - **Peter's Instruction: Resting in God's Grace**
     - 1 Peter 1:13 - Be sober-minded, and hope in grace.

5. **Strength in God's Grace**
   - **Paul's Instruction to Timothy**
     - 2 Timothy 2:1 - Be strong in the grace found in Christ.
     - The need for continuous dependence on God's empowerment
   - **Analogies of Endurance**
     - Soldier, athlete, and farmer (2 Timothy 2:3-6)
     - Each requires focus, discipline, and persever-

Chapter 10 Outline: Remain in Grace

ance.

- **Character and Grace**
  - Integrity is crucial for sustaining God's work.
  - Poor character can hinder the flow of grace to others.
  - Aligning our lives with God's grace allows His work to flourish.

6. **Living in the Overflow of God's Grace**

   - **Acts 4:33 - Great Grace upon the Church**
     - The body of Christ thrives when each believer contributes their grace.

   - **Philippians 1:5-7 - Partaking in Grace Together**
     - Sharing in grace strengthens relationships and unity.

   - **Faith and Expectation for More of God's Grace**
     - Churches become places of revival and impact through grace.

About the Author

Merle Shenk serves as the international director of DOVE International, a worldwide family of churches and ministries, and he is also the lead pastor at Newport Church. With a passion for discipleship, leadership development, and empowering followers of Jesus, Merle has dedicated his life to equipping believers to walk in their God-given purpose by the power of the Holy Spirit. He has over 20 years of pastoral ministry and leadership experience in cross-cultural contexts. In addition to this book *Great Grace*, Merle is also a co-author of the book, *Encountering the Supernatural*.

Merle and his family have traveled and ministered in various nations. They lived in Cape Town, South Africa for an extended season as missionary church planters before moving to the USA in 2016. The seasons of sowing into evangelism, leadership and equipping believers to walk in the power of the Holy Spirit continue to be life messages of their ministry to others. Merle and his wife, Cheree, were married in 2000 and are parents to five children. They live in Lititz, Pennsylvania.

Check out Merle's blog and his podcast

visit dcfi.org/merle-and-cheree/

Another Resource by Merle Shenk

Encountering the Supernatural

Discover God's amazing presence and power for your life. Wherever you are in your spiritual journey, this book will place you on a path to a greater revelation of God's supernatural power in everyday life.

by Larry Kreider, Kevin Kazemi and Merle Shenk
220 pages: $12.99
eBook and audiobook available

Visit **store.dcfi.org** for many discounts!

Made in the USA
Columbia, SC
07 May 2025

57612872R00100